The Story Behind
The Little Red Book

AN INTRODUCTION TO THE 12 STEPS OF THE ALCOHOLICS ANONYMOUS RECOVERY PROGRAM.

The NICOLLET GROUP of ALCOHOLICS ANONYMOUS, located in Minneapolis, humbly dedicate to all alcoholic men and women, this interpretation of the A. A. 12-step program.

As uncontrolled drinkers we became "POWERLESS OVER ALCOHOL AND OUR LIVES HAD BECOME UNMANAGEABLE".

This A.A. program by which we effected our recovery is extremely simple; it would need little interpretation in itself, except for the fact it corrects a highly complicated disease which has lowered our physical resistance, distorted our thinking, and rendered us spiritually ill.

Few uncontrolled drinkers realize the danger of their position or the great extent to which the disease alcoholism can damage and deteriorate their minds and bodies. Few realize the full significance and effectiveness of our simple program without the help and cooperation of understanding members who have arrested their alcoholism.

We have no connection with organized religion, medicine or psychology. We have drawn upon certain therapeutic virtues from them all, however, and have moulded them into a Design for Living that has returned us to sobriety and restored us to a place of service and respect in society.

The A.A. program is designed for uncontrolled drinkers who sincerely desire permanent sobriety and are willing to go to any lengths to get it. Men or women interested in temporary sobriety are not ready for this program.

The ability to be honest is a most necessary requirement following the desire of the new member for rehabilitation. Willingness to get well, and belief in a POWER GREATER THAN OURSELVES to promote recovery, are essentials necessary to success.

Spiritual concepts must be embraced, but again we say they do not

The first page of what would become known as *The Little Red Book,* in its original typescript form, 1945. Mimeograph, courtesy Brown University archives.

The Story Behind
The Little Red Book

The Evolution of a Twelve Step Classic

Damian McElrath, D.H.E.

HAZELDEN®

Hazelden
Center City, Minnesota 55012
hazelden.org

ISBN: 978-1-61649-505-3 (pbk); 978-1-61649-569-9 (ebook)

Library of Congress Cataloging-in-Publication Data
is on file with the Library of Congress

Editor's notes:
Some names, details, and circumstances have been changed to protect the privacy of those mentioned in this publication.

This publication is not intended as a substitute for the advice of health care professionals.

Alcoholics Anonymous, AA, and the *Grapevine* are registered trademarks of Alcoholics Anonymous World Services, Inc.

18 17 16 15 14   1 2 3 4 5 6

Interior design and typesetting: Terri Kinne
Developmental editor: Sid Farrar
Production editor: Mindy Keskinen

Hazelden's *Legacy 12* publishing initiative enriches people's recovery with dynamic multimedia works that use rare original-source documents to bring Alcoholics Anonymous and Twelve Step history alive.

To my grandchildren,
Ben, Emily, Nicklaus, Megan, Anna, and Sarah—
who have brought delight and joy
beyond words into my life

Contents

Acknowledgments

I owe much to Glenn Chesnut, whose research and writings prompted me to explore the earliest expressions of AA spirituality through the writings of Richmond Walker and Ed Webster. His essays on the early printings of *The Little Red Book* pushed me to delve more deeply into that volume, and Webster's other writings as well, and recognize them for what they were: some of the best examples of the early workings of AA and its spirituality.

The first soundings in this exploratory journey were the Hazelden-Pittman Archives at Hazelden, the groundbreaking addiction treatment center in Minnesota. These archives, described briefly in chapter 6 of this book, contained ten printings of *The Little Red Book*, three copies of *Stools and Bottles*, two of *Our Devilish Alcoholic Personalities*, and one copy of the rare book *Bar Room Reveries*. Box 49 contains copies of Ed Webster's letters to and from the cofounders of Alcoholics Anonymous, Dr. Bob and Bill W. Box 77 contains material related to the Nicollet Club, including much correspondence to and from Barry Collins. The contents are in no particular order and must be combed for material related to a particular subject. I am most grateful to Barb Weiner, Hazelden librarian and archivist, for her assistance, especially for the suggestions that led me to sources that I would have overlooked otherwise. I am grateful also for her assistance in guiding me through the paperwork to procure a grant from the AA Heckman Endowed Fellowship Fund, which allowed me to visit the AA Archives in Akron, Ohio.

Gail La Croix, the retired archivist at the Akron AA Archives, was very helpful in alerting me to material in their collections relating to Ed Webster, especially his personal copy of the Big Book of *Alcoholics Anonymous* with its many annotations. She also pointed me toward the Dr. Robert H. Smith Archive at Brown University's Center for Alcohol and Addiction Studies. I am grateful also for the help provided by Jim Burns, the archivist/conservator at the Akron Archives.

Special thanks to David Lewis, MD, Professor Emeritus of Community Health and Medicine at Brown, and especially to Holly Snyder, PhD, for their help in obtaining a copy of the 1945 manuscript *An Interpretation of the Twelve Steps of Alcoholics Anonymous* from the Robert H. Smith Archive. Permission to publish the first page of this manuscript has been granted by the John Hay Library, Brown University.

The very important 1947 second printing of *The Little Red Book,* complete with annotations, fell into my hands quite by accident. Fred Holmquist, director of the Hazelden Renewal Center, discovered a copy at a book sale and purchased it for his own collection. When he heard about my work on *The Little Red Book* he offered it to me for my study and use. It has played a very significant role in the evolution of this volume. Unless otherwise noted, this second printing of *The Little Red Book* is the one cited throughout these pages.

My thanks to archivist Michelle Mirtz, who provided me with material relating to my work during my visit to New York. Of particular interest was the Bill Wilson correspondence noted in this volume, which revealed Bill W.'s evolving attitude toward *The Little Red Book* and its growing popularity.

A chance e-mail seeking information about Ed Webster led to the e-mail address of his daughter, Lavina Jane Kamiske. She considered the volume about her father long overdue and readily agreed to supply me with photographs and personal recollections.

Thanks also to Ken Ring and Jerry Oys, whose knowledge of the AA Archives in Minnesota helped guide me through AA's early history in that state.

Finally, I am grateful for the grant from the Heckman Endowed Fellowship Fund, which provided me with the opportunity to explore the AA Archives at Akron, Ohio.

Introduction

The Evolution of *The Little Red Book*

The Little Red Book, written by Ed Webster, was published in 1946 by Webster and his close friend Barry Collins. The first printed edition and its earlier versions went by the title *An Interpretation of the Twelve Steps of the Alcoholics Anonymous Program*. It was one of many informal educational tracts with the same title that had been circulating within AA communities throughout the country. Their purpose was to educate the growing numbers of alcoholics seeking knowledge of the program outlined in the book *Alcoholics Anonymous,* known popularly as the Big Book. Dr. Bob and Bill W., the cofounders of AA, felt that what they had discovered when they first met in 1935 should be passed on. For the first four years this took place by word of mouth, with "one alcoholic talking to another" about the personal experience of recovery. Akron, Ohio, Dr. Bob's home, and New York, Bill's home, were the principal centers from which the good news about recovery radiated.

These orally transmitted keys to recovery soon found a safe depository in the Big Book, published in 1939. Two years later, in March 1941, popular journalist Jack Alexander's complimentary article in the *Saturday Evening Post* prompted an extraordinary number of inquiries about the program from all over the United States, and AA meetings began to spread across the country.

Soon, some early members began to see the need for an instructional manual that would share and summarize in an abbreviated fashion the principles behind the Twelve Step program presented in the Big Book. One of the first of these was published by AA headquarters (referred to here as the New York Office) in April 1940 with the simple title *A.A.* This tract was composed of six articles that had appeared in the *Houston Press*, written by a newspaperman who had recently found his recovery in the Cleveland AA fellowship. It was intended for people who had little or no knowledge of the Big Book, could not afford one, or were intimidated by the sheer volume of material it contained.

As noted earlier, several versions of *An Interpretation of the Twelve Steps of AA* had already been circulating among AA groups in the early 1940s. One of these, a variant of that developed by the Detroit group, was printed and distributed by a Washington, D.C., group. Pat Cronin, an early AA member in Minnesota, developed his guide, called *Instructor's Outline*, to use in Minneapolis's first AA group, the Alano Club. Soon Cronin chose another attender, Ed Webster, to help instruct newcomers to this group, who were welcomed into separate "beginners' meetings" for a time, a practice taken from the first group in Cleveland, Ohio.

It was during this period that Webster began to develop his ideas for his own version of the *Interpretation*—ideas that came to fruition after he moved with some other members to form Minneapolis's second AA group, the Nicollet Club. Instead of covering all the Steps in just four lessons, as Cronin's and other versions of the *Interpretation* had, Webster's version eventually evolved into a small book with an introduction and ten chapters. Each Step had its own chapter, except Steps Six and Seven, which shared one chapter, and Eight and Nine, which shared another. While it shared the *Interpretation* title with other texts already circulating throughout the country, this was a substantively different, greatly expanded work.

Within a few years, the book became very popular throughout the United States and Canada. Webster's version of the *Interpretation,* which became *The Little Red Book* at the time of the 1949 printing, has a singular place in the early history of Alcoholics Anonymous.[1] Its purpose was to introduce the newcomer to the richness of a new life and improved personality that can be revealed by living the Twelve Steps. In the tradition of the previous interpretations, the language was clear and simple. Its core message, which attracted people from all over the world, was this: Recovery from alcoholism means incorporating into one's daily life the spiritual principles contained in the Twelve Steps; that is, restoring one's relationships with our true selves, with others, and with the God of our understanding.

Over the course of the two decades that the book remained in the hands of Ed Webster, he continued to make changes, clarifying his thinking as the twenty-one printings evolved.

Initially, Webster's *Interpretation* earned the support of AA's two founders, Dr. Bob and Bill W. After reading the original manuscript, Dr. Bob endorsed it wholeheartedly, encouraging people to buy it and personally sharing copies with friends. He insisted that copies be kept in the New York warehouse for purchase and distribution. In his early correspondence with Webster, Bill W. also seemed to react positively to the book, but as the years wore on, his enthusiasm for the book waned. Bill W.'s letters clearly express the evolution of his thoughts from approval to concern, not in regard to the book's contents, but because of its widespread acceptance as a standard text that had not been approved by the New York Office. The book's popularity added weight to his support of the formation of the Conference on Approved Literature, which would eventually determine the canon of books approved by the New York Office. One of these books, *Twelve Steps and Twelve Traditions,* was written by Bill W. and published in 1952 as AA's official interpretation of the Steps. Fortunately, *The Little Red Book* did not die at that point, but continued to attract many AA members who laid claim to it as their own spiritual Magna Carta.

The development of *The Little Red Book* in Minneapolis allows us to examine in chapters 1 and 2 the major personalities in early Minneapolis AA circles—Barry Collins, Pat Cronin, and Ed Webster—and the evolution of the Alano and Nicollet Clubs in the very early days of AA. The two groups had underlying differences about who could become a member of AA. Was the desire to stop drinking sufficient? The hard line the Nicollet Club took on this issue is implied in *The Little Red Book*.

The Little Red Book, in conjunction with parts of two other books by Ed Webster, *Stools and Bottles* and *Our Devilish Alcoholic Personalities*, provide clear insights into Webster's spirituality, which is discussed in part 3. Taken together with his correspondence with Dr. Bob and to a lesser extent with Bill W., they speak to the simplicity of a spirituality based upon the Twelve Steps. With Steps Three and Eleven in particular, Webster seeks to reconcile the compelling dichotomy of the relationships between God's will and man's will.

Webster's spirituality can be clearly discerned from his writings, especially from *The Little Red Book*. It is what I often refer to as "relational" spirituality, that is, it is to be found in the ordered relationships that we have with our true selves, with others, and with the God of our understanding. Each of the Steps points to one of those relationships.

With his continual reference to the alcoholic personality, Webster is pointing to the other person/self residing inside the alcoholic, who intends the individual no end of harm. Self-centered and disconnected from reality, it is this self whose pernicious influence does everything in its power to destroy the loving relationships we have with others. Finally, it corrupts and corrodes whatever our relationship with our Higher Power, the God of our understanding.

This alcoholic personality is the source of much mischief and misfortune. In contrast, the discovery of one's real personality provides the lodestone that directs life into finding those who wish to share our journey. Nurturing our real selves and cultivating relationships that will enrich our lives without the poison of alcohol puts us in a better position to explore our relationship with a God of our understanding.

One of the best early definitions of the AA Fellowship is that it is a nonprofessional, mutual help group of men and women organized for the purpose of helping each other lead sober and contented lives within the community and principles of Alcoholics Anonymous. People coming into the program needed to be taught the basic principles contained in the Twelve Steps. What evolved slowly in Minnesota (and elsewhere) were organized mutual help programs using the Fellowship as its basis, intended to supplement the educational elements of AA as passed on in the Big Book. This educational model, which eventually came to be called the

Minnesota Model, became the motivation for founding treatment facility prototypes using the Twelve Steps: Pioneer House, founded by Pat Cronin in 1948, and Hazelden Manor, founded by Cronin's sponsee, Lynn Carroll, in 1949. Both Cronin and Carroll simply wanted to provide an environment for those who needed more time to immerse themselves in the study of the Big Book and the Steps and their practical application. Lectures on the Twelve Steps, related topics, and subsequent discussions were the heart of the program. Essentially, Cronin and Carroll were taking the principles of mutual help and delivering them in a safe environment.

Gradually the original Twelve Step mutual help paradigm transitioned into professional treatment programs like the Hazelden Betty Ford Foundation, with a multidisciplinary staff and integrated treatment programs for addiction to alcohol and other drugs, as well as co-occurring mental health disorders. In tracing the history of *The Little Red Book*, we are reminded of what it was like in the beginning of the AA movement, when all we had was a simple and untarnished approach to recovery based on the Twelve Step program documented in AA's Big Book.

The popularity of Webster's *Interpretation*, first published as a book in 1946, and Richmond Walker's "Little Black Book," are excellent barometers of how serious the early recovering community was about the message and simplicity of recovery. Almost half of Walker's book traces itself back to talks that he gave to a variety of groups in the Boston area in 1944 and 1945. They are great examples of the early and simple expectations of AA members, the importance of the Big Book, and the program that it presented. The same can be said of the lectures on all the Steps that Webster was giving at the Nicollet Group (1944–1946): Read the Big Book, practice these principles, attend meetings, and implement the Twelfth Step through service to others. This is what *The Little Red Book* eventually encapsulated. This book has played a central role in distilling and disseminating the kernels of the spiritual principles contained in the Twelve Steps. In doing so, it brought an important measure of consistency and discipline to the educational role of the early AA Fellowship.[2]

PART I

The Backdrop for
The Little Red Book

Much can be learned from the early years of AA as people, clubs, and pamphlets converge to form a colorful tapestry, creating an interesting and compelling history of Alcoholics Anonymous. Further, it serves as a meditation on the dialectic between continuity and change, between "what it was like before . . . and what it is like now."

■ ■ ■

Alcoholics Anonymous Comes to Minnesota

BARRY COLLINS AND PAT CRONIN

There's a triumvirate of people in the Minnesota mix whose interconnected lives provide the necessary backdrop to the events leading to the publication of *The Little Red Book*. Barry Collins, Pat Cronin, and Ed Webster are important figures in the early history of AA in Minneapolis and elsewhere in Minnesota, the Midwest, and Canada. Two of them, Collins and Webster, play important roles in the origins of the Nicollet Club from which *The Little Red Book* emerged.

Barry Collins

Barry Collins figures prominently as one of the most important members of AA in the program's early history in Minnesota. He is probably one of the least known to subsequent generations. Chan Forman was a very close friend of Collins. Seven months before he met Pat Cronin in November 1940, Forman, a recovering alcoholic in the recently formed Chicago group, had written a three and a half page letter to Collins.[1] In it he recalled their old drinking days together

11

and more importantly his own recovery—"what it was like, what happened, and what it is like now." He described the Chicago men as "an informal group of ex-guzzlers." The letter then goes on to describe how his drinking had been increasing dangerously until a newspaper friend from the previously mentioned group "started working on him" and introduced him to the group, which had been started in Chicago about a year before by an "alumnus" of the Cleveland group. It now had about fifty members, an interesting cross section of Chicago, including several newspaper men, salesmen, firemen, a detective, a lawyer, two doctors, and a dentist—"every last one of them an alcoholic." Forman told Collins that the surprising thing is "that the damn thing works."

Forman continued, writing that in a couple of weeks he and some others from the Chicago group were driving to Minneapolis to meet with four persons interested in quitting drinking. (Actually the couple of weeks turned into half a year.) The plan was to get them together and tell them how the Chicago group worked. He then told Collins about the Big Book and urged him to buy a copy, or he could send him one. Along with the letter, Forman sent Collins a pamphlet published by the Alcoholic Foundation with the simple title "AA."

The reply to Forman's letter came not from Collins but from his wife, Corrine, who wrote that Forman was a little late with his proposed "cure" for Collins. He was in the hospital and if he survived he would not be able to drink again. "The Doctor told him so." Nonetheless, Forman's letter came at the right time. Collins was ready to change. When Collins was released from the hospital, the letter and the information about AA provided the necessary lifeline as well as a life calling.

On the occasion of Collins's twenty-seventh sobriety anniversary, Forman reminded those gathered to honor Collins: "Soon you (Collins) were talking AA to nurses, doctors or anybody else who would listen and you were making converts among the non-alcoholics. . . Everybody out there in Minneapolis, and in towns north, south, and west knows the rest of your story. How you got out of the hospital, refused to become an invalid, and started to carry the message far and wide. How you sponsored drunk after drunk after drunk. Your success was astounding! Somehow you were able to persuade one suffering drunk after another that this program would work for him, show him how to go about it, and inspire him to do it."

"Meanwhile I would get the word by the grapevine—and I don't mean the magazine—of your missionary work in town after town in Minnesota, out in South Dakota and points west and as far north as the arctic drinking town of Flin Flon. A long, long chain of recoveries that will go on and on."[2]

Indeed, Collins's energy was inexhaustible. Despite his periodic hospitalizations, he continued to do an incredible amount of Twelfth Stepping while he was vice president of the Alano Club (April 1972), where, for the next year and a half, he worked closely with Pat Cronin in spreading the message of recovery. Collins worked hard practicing the Twelfth Step, supporting "the mother club" and serving as a model of recovery. He was no less instrumental in the growth of the club than Cronin, who was well aware of the valuable role that Collins played. As Cronin wrote to his fellow Minneapolis AAs, "Many of you, perhaps, don't know it but Barry C. was the first practicing AA in Minneapolis . . . Only the fact that he was hopelessly invalided for a long time prevented Barry from getting out and organizing. You all know what he has accomplished since he has been able to get around. That guy has more ideas in five minutes than I have in five weeks, and we all owe him a note of thanks. . ."[3]

Pat Cronin

Most people acquainted with the history of AA in Minnesota know the story of Pat Cronin being visited by two members of AA from Chicago—Bill Long and Chan Forman. They had been given the names of four people who were looking for help but they were only able to find one, and that was Pat Cronin. After attending the Minnesota-Michigan football game on Saturday, November 9, 1940, they "barged in on"

Cronin and spent the rest of the day and evening talking about the Big Book, the Twelve Steps, and the path to recovery. Then the Armistice Day Blizzard stranded them in the Twin Cities, giving them more time "to work on Cronin." His sobriety date was November 11, 1940.

Years later when telling his story at an AA meeting, Cronin remembered writing to Forman and telling him how worried he was about getting through Christmas and New Year's. Forman's response was simply not to worry about those two days, as they might never come. "Be concerned only with today," he urged. "I think that is what put me over—the knowledge that I did not have to quit for the rest of my life, that one day at a time would do it."[4] (It is interesting that neither New York nor Forman alerted him to the recovery and presence of Collins.) Cronin took the advice to heart and included the phrase "Take one day at a time" at the end of the Twelve Step instructor's outline that he is said to have helped develop for the Minneapolis Alano Club, a group that he had helped found. Cronin recalled that in February 1941, New York informed him about the article on AA by Jack Alexander that was being published in the March issue of the *Saturday Evening Post.* The magazine wouldn't hit newsstands for three weeks, but Cronin immediately went to the local magazine distributor and ordered 100 copies. He paid for them with a five-dollar bill (at that time the magazine cost only a nickel). As the mail came into the New York Office in response to the articles, the secretary sent any names of people from Minnesota to Pat Cronin.[5] On his own initiative, Cronin went to a local newspaper columnist, Cedric Adams of the *Star Journal,* with a copy of the *Post* article and asked him to put a line in his column asking anyone who read the article and wanted to join AA should write to AA in care of Adams's column. Adams guaranteed that he would turn them over to the local chapter, "which was me (Cronin)." The mail came in by the bushel but much of it, Cronin acknowledged, was from "wives, mothers, and Aunt Minnie." He went on, "Nevertheless I got enough letters from men and women so that I got started among strangers. When they found out that I had been dry from the preceding November, I got it made."[6]

A month later, in April, Cronin had a group of six members whose interest and knowledge of the program varied greatly. He rented two rooms at 200 East Franklin Ave. in Minneapolis, and later rented three more. Ed Webster recalls that at the end of the year he was fortunate to become part of a squad of desperate "last gaspers" who relied entirely on studying the message in *Alcoholics Anonymous* wherein he learned the working mechanics of the Twelve Steps. "Fundamental instructions relative to the application of the Twelve Steps became necessary as our membership increased. Some members didn't own Big Books; other members qualified as alcoholics (according to Step Number One) but skipped the rest of the Steps, except that part of Step Twelve, which says to carry the message to alcoholics. Their ignorance of the AA program gave them but little message to carry."[7]

—

The Alano and Nicollet Clubs

The early history of these two clubs provides us with insights into the diversity of ideas regarding the maintenance of recovery. In a sense the two clubs represent two different emerging traditions—Alano, the more ecumenical tradition of New York and Bill W., and Nicollet, the more conservative tradition of Akron and Dr. Bob. Articles on "slips and slippers" occupied the pages of the early issues of the *Grapevine*. Unconditional surrender on one's knees had no place for slips. In the Big Book, page 58, Webster would have replaced the words "*Rarely* have we seen a person fail" with "*Never* have we seen a person fail."

The Alano Club

With the surge in membership at the new AA club Cronin had started on Franklin Avenue, the group needed larger quarters. A Certificate of Incorporation of the Alano Society of Minneapolis, Inc. was filed April 7, 1942. Pat Cronin was listed as president while Mary M. Barnd and B. N. Collins were vice presidents. That same month, the property at 2218 First Avenue South was purchased from the Washburn family for nineteen thousand dollars. A stipulation of the deed was that a part of 2218 was to be kept in its original form. It is referred to as "the mother club." At that time the club had 135 members.

Aside from the need for a larger meeting space, the club still had to address questions about the nature of the program and the spiritual principles found within the Twelve Steps. Pat Cronin's own intense three-to-four-day novitiate and initiation into AA was unique. It was unlikely that other newcomers to the program would have the spiritual experience of the 1940 blizzard. Theirs would be of the educational variety. Someone had to act as "educator," an all-consuming task that fell to Cronin. He may have had as an initial instructional guide the booklet that Ruth Hock sent to him on August 15, 1940. Commiserating with his loneliness, she added at the end of the letter: "We are enclosing a copy of a booklet recently published by the Alcoholic Foundation, which in the absence of the book itself, gives a clear though brief outline of our work and methods."[1] This may well have been another copy of the same booklet, "AA" published by The Alcoholic Foundation, a companion piece to the Big Book that Chan Forman sent to Barry Collins in April 1940. This early tract was composed of six articles that appeared in the *Houston Press* written by a newspaperman who had recently found his recovery in the Cleveland AA Fellowship. Classes for his ragtag group began sometime in

1941 and, initially, they probably occurred over four consecutive days. As membership grew and the group settled at the Alano Club at 2218 First Avenue South, the presentations became more formalized and occurred for an hour one day a week over a four-week period. It was during this time that a more formal instructor's outline was composed. The four-week course was divided as follows: the first week dealt with Step One; the second week, Steps Four, Five, Eight, and Nine; the third week, Steps Two, Three, Five, Six, Seven, and Eleven; and the fourth week, Steps Ten and Twelve. This division of the Steps aligns very closely with the manuals and "interpretations" created by other groups across the country that were soon to come. What is interesting about the Alano presentation is that Step 5 is repeated twice—a formula different from the Step manuals employed by other groups.

Since the instructor's manual does mention the existence of the Alano Club, it was probably put together by Cronin sometime after April 1942, and may have been one of the earliest of the training manuals.

The Nicollet Club

The first Founders' Day Banquet, sponsored by the Alano Club, was held in November 1942, and was attended by 237 recovering people, friends, and family. A year later the Club at 2218 had 200 members, including a dozen women. But then the following month members of the Alano Club were surprised and saddened to learn that thirteen members who had been meeting at the home of Manus McFadden planned to leave the Alano Club and establish their own group. This new group, which came to be known as the Nicollet Club of Alcoholics Anonymous, included Barry Collins and Ed Webster. Initially, the group rented rooms at Eleventh Street and Nicollet Avenue over Hedemark's Restaurant. Then in November 1945, the club moved to a newly renovated and attractive space at Nicollet and Lake Street. At this time the Articles of Incorporation and bylaws were adopted.[2]

It is not easy to get a handle on precisely why the break occurred. There are many sources that point to some general dissatisfaction about the way that the Alano Club was run. It also appears that the members who were divorcing themselves from the Alano Club were unhappy with what they felt was the lenient manner in which new members were accepted into the club, some of whom they felt were not truly alcoholic. Years later Webster wrote in *Bulletin 13* (Vol. III, 1953), a newsletter put out by members of the Nicollet Club: "Non-alcoholic drinkers in A.A. soon find that our Twelve Step Therapy prescribes beyond their needs. Not being compulsive drinkers, contented sobriety is neither a matter of life nor death for them. They are just disillusioned people who are trying to set bones that are not broken. The few who possess the rare faculty of open mindedness and ability to profit by the mistakes of others may avoid breaking them.

We do not predict but wish them well." In another paragraph Webster wrote: "Since *Bulletin 13*'s primary function is 'to carry the message to alcoholics' other drinkers may consider our treatment of the program too rigorous and exacting. For them this may be true."[3]

Nor was the Nicollet group happy with the manner in which the Alano group was dealing with those who relapsed, the so-called "slippers." "Slipping is unnecessary and will not be tolerated at Nicollet." The Nicollet group was displeased with Alano's poor screening process, which seemed to allow meeting attendees who did not have the real desire to stop drinking or who were therefore not really powerless.

The Nicollet group employed the term "real alcoholics" in contrast to those who were dancing around recovery. "AA is for alcoholics only; we cannot help others (potential alcoholics, heavy drinkers, etc.,) who are only looking for a means to get off the hook."[4] Further, "some people reason that although they are not alcoholic, alcoholism could be avoided by belonging to an A.A. group. This is questionable for it is not until the alcoholic has severely punished himself and his family that he gives serious thought to the arresting of his alcoholism."[5] This eventually would conflict with the Third Tradition, which states, "The only requirement for A.A. membership is a desire to stop drinking."

This doctrinaire approach was probably behind reports of bickering among committee members about rules as a source of frustration. It is interesting that in September 1945, Bill W. wrote an article for the *Grapevine* in which he took to task the "rule makers" and their need for rules: "Were we to proceed by rules, somebody would have to make them and, more difficult still, somebody would have to enforce them. 'Rule-making' has often been tried. It usually results in controversy among the 'rule makers' as to what the rules should be. . ."[6]

The Nicollet group also stood out in emphasizing the importance of the family, and wives were expected to attend the meetings with their husbands. In this sense, the Nicollet group was one of the first nonofficial family programs in the country.

In the notes drawn up in preparation for a booklet celebrating the twentieth anniversary of the Nicollet Club in 1964, it is stated: "[at the meetings we] talk about the Big Book and our brand of AA. If they want to water it down they are welcome to go to other groups where this is the practice," further, "all answers are in the Big Book with help from *The Little Red Book*. These are the only references to be used when conducting a group meeting. The proper indoctrination of the new members occurs through Step classes, generally two sessions a year—Spring and Fall."[7] These classes had to be taken before the new member could participate in the regular meetings, at which time he would be given a key to the clubhouse.

The departure of the Alano members for the Nicollet Club was a painful experience for all. It also may have been one of the first splinters of a group since Cleveland separated from Akron. Although feelings may have been hurt, as they were when the Clevelanders departed, principles prevailed above personalities, and the documents indicate no acrimony, suspicions of betrayal, or recriminations tossed at one another. Early on, however, the Nicollet group did compete with the Alano group for new members. Responding to Collins's request for the names of potential AA members, the secretary, Bobbie Burgher, replied that the New York office took an evenhanded approach in sorting out those who sought help from the Minneapolis area.

Barry Collins was a go-getter and competitor and wanted to establish the Nicollet Club as one of the leading AA groups in the country, a primus inter pares, one level lower than Akron and New York, especially since the Club's mimeographed *Interpretation* was beginning to register a favorable response, particularly in Canada. Also, he was eager to have Bill W. visit the Nicollet Club, as it would signal his blessing and an endorsement of the Club's direction.

Between the years 1944 and 1947, the members of the Nicollet group established a recreational event called The AA Founder's Retreat. Barry Collins sent invitations to AA groups throughout the country, and while overall response was slim, the invitations cast a wide net geographically. For example, Collins invited the leaders from Winnipeg, Dallas, Oklahoma, St. Louis, Peoria, Chicago, Toledo, Cleveland, Detroit, New Jersey, New York, Vermont, Boston, Toronto, and Salt Lake City. The event was by invitation only and invitations were sent to those who were considered to be the founders of groups.

When Collins wrote to a recovering friend from the New York area, asking whether he could prevail upon Bill W. and his wife to attend the Founder's Day Retreat sponsored by Nicollet, the friend replied that it would be easier if the invitation would include spending time with the Alano Club (also called by its address, "2218"). Bill W., the friend explained, always felt obligated to visit all groups in an area in which he was to make an appearance and would be reluctant to spend a week with the Nicollet Club and little to no time at 2218. Bill W. did not make any of the four retreats, while Dr. Bob made two.[8]

Those attending one or the other of the outings included Earl Treat, the first AA member in Chicago and the author of the Big Book story "He Sold Himself Short"; Ernie Gerig, one of the first members in Toledo, Ohio; Arch Trowbridge, the first AA member in Detroit and author of the Big Book story "The Man Who Mastered Fear"; and Pere Edgar, the first AA member in Winnipeg, Canada. Dr. Bob attended the first and third of the outings. He fished, played bridge, took walks "and wasn't aloof at all. He was very approachable if you wanted to talk to him." On one occasion "it was April and cold in Minnesota. Ernie and Ruth G. who stayed with Doc and Anne in one of the unheated cabins, recalled that they slept with their coats on, and on one particularly bitter morning, Dr. Bob sprinkled his chest with water and said that was going to be the extent of his sprucing up for that day."[9]

But the Founder's Day Retreat was to be short-lived. After the fourth outing, dwindling attendance convinced Collins to abandon the retreats. Some speculated the retreat ended "because it was not open to all and was thus against AA policy."[10]

The Nicollet group members could seem exclusive at times as well. "The annual fishing trips, however, created some problems for the Nicollet group. Someone would ask 'Are you going on the fishing trip?' Often the response would be 'No, I haven't been invited.' While the trips were presumably open to all, it seems that more than a few Nicollet members did not feel free to attend unless specifically invited. By the time the [final] trip had taken place, the event was discontinued, the feeling being it had become divisive."[11]

Another observer close to the scene was the Rev. Forrest Richeson, who worked with alcoholics in his position as a spiritual leader. "The real essence of the struggle between Pat Cronin and Barry Collins evolved around the issue as to whether or not AA was for everybody," Richeson wrote.

"Cronin's concept was that it was for everyone and fully open and inclusive (Tradition Three). Collins took an exclusive point of view and placed the emphasis on couples and their families. His approach excluded as often as it included. It is well for Minnesota AA that the concept of Pat Cronin predominated in the region."[12]

The Nicollet Club and Dr. Bob

The Nicollet group had a very close relationship with Dr. Bob, which, as we'll see, was to have a major impact on the eventual acceptance and dissemination of *The Little Red Book*. The intention of the Nicollet group was to pattern their meetings after the original King School Group in Akron, Ohio, for which Dr. Bob was the inspiration. The strong links of this relationship were forged during the outings and through correspondence between Dr. Bob, Collins, and Webster, which, along with Dr. Bob's affection for *The Little Red Book*, suggest a common understanding regarding spirituality.

Before he met Bill W., Dr. Bob's search for God began when he attended Oxford Group meetings. There he learned about the Four Absolutes—honesty, unselfishness, love, and purity—that he used as yardsticks against which he would measure his decisions to do the right thing. He was impressed with the group because they seemed happy, but he did not sense at any time that the Oxford teachings/meetings were

Dr. Bob (left) visits the Nicollet Club in the mid-1940s.
With him are Earl Treat (center) and Barry Collins.

the answer to his alcohol problems. Dr. Bob never had a "white flash" spiritual experience, as Bill W. described. What he did learn from Bill W. was the spirituality of service—"the giving of one's effort and strength and time." Service and surrender were the underpinnings of his spirituality.

Under Dr. Bob's spiritual direction, newcomers to AA were to express their surrender by "getting down on their knees" and humbly asking God to remove all shortcomings. Even if the phrase "getting down on one's knees" was later removed from the Seventh Step, Dr. Bob continued its practice. He "was wonderful at getting surrenders."[13] Bill W. and Dr. Bob made Bill D., the third member of AA—the "Man on the Bed"—"get down on his knees at the side of the bed right there in the hospital and pray and say that he would turn his life over to God. This spiritual exercise was essential to Dr. Bob's spiritual process in helping others."[14]

Service and surrender were Dr. Bob's spiritual couplet. The Nicollet group inherited this couplet from Dr. Bob, which they expressed by making *The Little Red Book* available to others as a form of sponsorship and the practice of the Twelfth Step. Dr. Bob, who felt the Big Book was too complicated for many newcomers, wanted some "Blue Collar" AA pamphlets for the Fellowship[15]—a reason for his hearty endorsement of the Nicollet's version of the *Interpretation* developed by Webster and its later iteration as *The Little Red Book.*

Dr. Bob's last words to the Fellowship, spoken on Sunday, July 30, 1950, were:

> And one more thing: None of us would be here today if somebody hadn't taken time to explain things to us, to give a little pat on the back, to take us to a meeting or two, to do numerous little kind and thoughtful acts in our behalf. So let us never get such a degree of smug complacency that we're not willing to extend to our less fortunate brothers that help which has been so beneficial to us.[16]

As long as Dr. Bob lived he remained Nicollet's model and spiritual guide, providing support to Webster, who was composing and editing his *Interpretation*.

Ed Webster and the Origins of
The Little Red Book

Edward A. Webster was born March 21, 1892 and died June 3, 1971 at the age of seventy-nine with twenty-four years of sobriety, which he dedicated to helping other alcoholics find recovery. He was survived by his wife Hazel B., a son Fred A., daughter Mrs. James (Lavina) Kamiske, and brother Terrance L. Webster.

Webster wrote his own very general autobiographical sketch in the Introduction to *Our Devilish Alcoholic Personalities,* which was published in 1970, the year before he died. Much of this chapter is based upon portions of that work as well as information provided by his daughter.[1] He begins by remarking that he was born "cold sober" in the small town of Eau Galle in northern Wisconsin. His parents were serious, dedicated Christians for whom drinking was a "cardinal sin," bars "dens of iniquity," and those who frequented them "immoral and undesirable citizens." He had two brothers, only one of whom, Terrence, survived him. In high school he excelled in wrestling, a skill he occasionally used after graduation when unreasonably provoked. He states that he left home and religion at the age of eighteen.

He served in the United States Navy twice, once before World War I, then reenlisting after the outbreak of that war.

Ed Webster in his dapper youth,
probably shortly before World War I.

In between he went to work with Union Carbide. When World War I began, he enlisted again, and he was assigned to a battleship that patrolled the Atlantic Ocean.

After his discharge from the navy he met his future wife, Hazel Blanche Wagner in Chicago, Illinois, where he was working and she was going to college. She was born in White Lake, South Dakota, in 1893. They were married in Minneapolis on May 29, 1920. The Websters were Scotch and English and his wife's family was part Irish. Ed and his two brothers, Terrence and Lloyd, were very personable, each with a great sense of humor. The family reunions were loud and boisterous, with lots of laughter and teasing from the three brothers.

Ed and Hazel had two children, a son, Fred, and a daughter, Jane Lavina. Ed was very strict with his children, and he was particularly hard on his son. His son pushed back against his father's controlling manner, while his daughter was always looking for ways to please and avoid confrontation.

Upon his discharge after the war, he returned to his old job with Union Carbide but was reassigned to a subsidiary called Linde Air Products, where he worked until he retired in 1960.

He sold welding equipment and several types of gases, including oxygen for hospitals. He had a little workshop in the basement of his home that was full of oxygen tanks and welding tools. He became an excellent welder, a talent that allowed him to give great sales presentations, and he was a talented carpenter who built attractive and sturdy furniture. As a handyman he could fix just about anything. He was also an avid gardener and later in his life, during World War II, he planted a huge victory garden to keep his neighbors supplied with vegetables and fruits of all kinds.

In the years following his discharge, Webster was drinking a lot, and the fact that he didn't lose his job during the Great Depression speaks to his extraordinary sales skills. His sense of humor was another reason for his success as a salesman. It later proved a valuable asset in coaxing other drunks not to take themselves too seriously. He made friends easily and kept them forever. Everyone seemed to like him. If there were disagreements, he was always called upon to be the middleman, the "negotiator" who brought about "harmony," a theme that appears prominently throughout *The Little Red Book.*

Ed Webster in the 1950s.

It was said that Webster could sell anybody anything. His work took him through much of the United States and through parts of Canada. Access to a large expense account for the entertainment of his customers contributed to his success. Alcohol gradually became a very close traveling companion. In his initial years he had an excellent sales record, which also "prevented him from facing the fact that he was seldom sober." He sought what became known as the "geographical cure" for his problem by transferring to another territory. But eventually it all caught up with him and a ten-day tango with alcohol cost him the temporary loss of his job at the end of 1941.

All this time, his long-suffering wife, Hazel, had tried everything to get him to stop drinking. This was before AA and well before Al-Anon became a staple for the family recovery process. She nagged, cried, prayed, threatened, but nothing worked. The family minister told her that she must not be praying hard enough or her husband would have stopped drinking. That's when her search for help expanded to other churches, including a charismatic congregation that practiced speaking in tongues. Webster's drinking hurt his wife deeply, but never entirely disrupted their relationship. After he got sober, their relationship continued to strengthen and deepen over the years.

But in late 1941, when Hazel was feeling as if she had exhausted all possibilities, she came across the Jack Alexander article about AA in the *Saturday Evening Post*. At the time, AA was quite new in Minnesota, but on December 11, 1941, she made the call. She remembers that two scruffy-looking men appeared at their home and had Ed hospitalized. Upon discharge he learned about an AA Club House, the first floor of a tiny five-room apartment on Park Avenue in Minneapolis, where he would meet Pat Cronin for the first time. (It was the flat where some of the Dillinger gang had allegedly made their last stand against the Minneapolis police.)

It was very much a hit-or-miss operation that year as Cronin, without much help, was trying to instruct the newcomers and send others with some months of sobriety and a little knowledge of the Twelfth Step to help those like Ed Webster. Things got better the following year when a permanent home for the clubhouse was established at 2218 First Avenue South in Minneapolis. It was thereafter called the Alano Club. Along with his sobriety, Ed's relationship with his wife continued to improve, and eventually Hazel became a strong AA supporter. She attended the Nicollet Club meetings faithfully after Ed started going there.

It was at the Alano Club that Webster first met Barry Collins, who, as vice president of the club, worked closely with Cronin. Collins was known for his talent to get things done, and he and Webster became lifelong friends. As their friendship deepened, Collins would often drop by Webster's home unannounced to discuss current AA matters, the time of their next fishing trip, or when it was convenient to visit Dr. Bob. While they had different personalities, they danced to the same AA tune. Collins was somewhat reserved, some even called him aloof, giving off an air of superiority. He was by nature a leader with the ability to cut through the details and get things done. He and Webster were both deeply committed to AA and to the implementation of Step Twelve, which was the bedrock of the Nicollet Club model that they and others would later establish.

As membership grew at the new Alano Club, Cronin's presentations on the Twelve Steps were formalized and bundled together into what was called the Instructor's Outline. Presented one day a week over a four-week period, this outline was gradually replaced with what would become *An Interpretation of the Twelve Steps,* which Cronin had developed. At first Cronin took it upon himself to personally conduct all the classes. Soon, however, he was groaning under the burden of the large influx of new members and facetiously lamented that if he did not get help soon he would be led to drink. He himself organized a pool of volunteers from whom he selected those who were ready to carry on this important work. He then trained them as presenters for his version of *An Interpretation of the Twelve Steps.*

Webster was one of those chosen. He seemed an ideal selection because of his salesmanship and the caring and considerate nature with which he completed his Twelfth

Step work. He wrote that his selection "appealed to my alcoholic ego, of course, but it demanded a close study of the manner in which the book *Alcoholics Anonymous* suggested the Steps should be lived. Since one cannot impart to another something he does not understand himself, I compiled notes from which I gave lectures on all of the Twelve Steps."

Thus began his work on his own version of the *Interpretation*. Other versions, for example, the one used in Washington, D.C., were divided into four sections, each containing multiple Steps with the exception of Step One, which stood alone. In contrast, Webster's *Interpretation* dealt with each Step individually, except Steps Six and Seven, and Eight and Nine, which were treated as couplets.

As Webster's lectures evolved, visitors to Nicollet, including people from Western Canada, expressed a keen interest in having printed copies of his notes. Webster felt his original notes were useless to other members without further clarification, so he expanded and edited them. In a letter (no longer extant) to Bobbie Burgher at the New York Office, Collins appeared to be asking indirectly if it would be appropriate for Nicollet to be selling copies of the talks that Webster was putting together, just as Washington, D.C. was doing. Burgher wrote that New York favored the tradition of groups writing their own "can openers" (pamphlets), and any group that wished to purchase them should feel free to do so. Instead of buying the popular Washington pamphlet, Collins and Webster went ahead and mimeographed Webster's talks on the Steps and began selling them to those AA individuals and groups who wished to use them.[2]

They became increasingly popular and, as early as 1945, were being used by groups in Canada with which Nicollet had forged some very strong bonds. The original Winnipeg group, started in January 1945, "met twice weekly and acquired a copy of the manuscript. . . . By the summer of 1945 the young Manitoba group had 13 members."[3] Members of the Nicollet group carried the message to many AA groups in Canada, which were struggling to get started, in addition to Winnipeg, Port Arthur, Thunder Bay, Assiniboine, and Flin Flon, among others.

In the introduction to the 1946 first printing of Webster's *Interpretation* in book form, which carried the title *Interpretation of The Twelve Steps of the Alcoholics Anonymous Program*, the Author's Note reads: "This book was originally prepared as a series of notes for Twelve-Step discussions for new A.A. members. It proved to be very effective and helpful. Many groups adopted it, using mimeographed copies. . ." These mimeographed copies of the lectures served as the text from which the newer members could follow what was being taught. One of these still survives. Dated "Revised, 6-5-45" it is titled "An Introduction to the Twelve Steps of the Alcoholics Anonymous Recovery Program." The first paragraph contains the lines that distinguish this mimeographed printing from the first edition of the book, which was printed a year later. (It wasn't until the 1949 edition that the title was changed to *The Little Red Book*). It reads: "The Nicollet Group of Alcoholics Anonymous, located in Minneapolis, humbly dedicate to all alcoholic men and women this interpretation of the A.A. Twelve Step program." As the popularity of Webster's Nicollet *Interpretation* continued to increase, Webster and Collins decided it was time to print/publish the mimeographed text. "The demand for this Interpretation in book form from both individuals and groups made printing advisable." There is ample evidence that they kept in touch with Dr. Bob about the progress of the project. Looking back in 1970, Webster wrote: "In 1946 my friend Barry C. drove to Akron, Ohio, leaving the manuscript of 'The Little Red Book' with Doctor Bob who wrote shortly afterwards that he thought the book would be most helpful to our members."[4]

In 1946, Dr. Bob attended the third Founder's Day Retreat, sponsored by the Nicollet group, where Webster may have told Dr. Bob about the popularity of the mimeographed *Interpretation* and his thoughts about publishing it. In November 1946, when it was finally published, he wrote to Webster in his laconic style that he found the book to be "quite alright," and the following month elaborated that he "enjoyed your little book very much & know that it will prove to be a lot of help to many."[5] In subsequent correspondence between Webster and Dr. Bob, Dr. Bob expressed his interest in the book and told of the times he had given the book to others. Although Dr. Bob wrote little compared to Bill W., we can extrapolate that the publication of what became *The Little Red Book* embodies Dr. Bob's interpretation of the Twelve Steps while the AA book, *Twelve Steps and Twelve Traditions*, conveys Bill W.'s.

Webster considered the publication and distribution of the book as Nicollet's way of implementing the Twelfth Step in the form of "long range sponsorship." Dr. Bob thought so highly of it that he insisted that copies of it be kept in the New York warehouse where it could be more easily distributed.

In her book, *Language of the Heart*, Trysh Travis is of the same mind as G. Chesnut that the *Interpretation* and *The Little Red Book*, "is the closest thing we have as to how Dr. Bob taught newcomers how to work the Twelve Steps." It best expressed what is "the traditional" spirituality of the Midwest literature—surrender to God, through quiet time, insistence on an orderly and early working of the Steps, and service to the AA Fellowship.[6]

PART II

The Conceptual Evolution and Printing History of *The Little Red Book*

An Interpretation of the Twelve Steps of the Alcoholics Anonymous Program was self-published by Barry Collins and Ed Webster under the publisher's name Coll-Web in book form in August 1946. The date of publication was listed as August MCMXLVI (1946). Later on we shall see why it was important to capture the year of publication in its Roman numeral form.

■ ■ ■

The historical and conceptual development of *The Little Red Book* can be divided into three stages. The first stage, from 1946 until 1949, covers the first five printings; the second stage, from 1950 until 1967, extends to the twenty-first printing; and in the third and final stage, the Hazelden Foundation purchases the copyright to the book and publishes the fiftieth anniversary edition in 1996.

Stage I: 1946–1949

In his article "The First Edition of The Little Red Book," Glenn Chesnut taps into many sources and covers this first stage of this development with his usual attention to detail. He leaves us with some thoughts as to why knowledge of this period is so important for the history of AA.[1] He writes, "We could describe *The Little Red Book* as the best compendium around of what Dr. Bob and his circle in the upper Midwest regarded as the most important things to teach newcomers." He points out how the title by which the book is presently known evolved: "The early printings had a dark ruby red cover, so it came to be known affectionately by its users as 'The Little Red Book,' to distinguish it from the book *Alcoholics Anonymous*, which originally was called the "big red book" because of its red and yellow cover. The 1949 edition (printing) had the title 'The Little Red Book,' the name which carried through to the present day."

The remainder of the article addresses the changes found in the printings that followed the original 1946 edition: two printings in 1947, a fourth printing in 1948, and the two versions of the 1949 printing. In the first version, printed in 1949, the text on page 62 was upside down, which was corrected by pasting a page over it. In a second 1949 printing, that page was corrected. Chesnut believes that the 1949 edition "Should be taken as a kind of benchmark version for many purposes since this was the last edition where Dr. Bob had any input into the book."

What input Dr. Bob had in the printings subsequent to the original one is not clear. In correspondence between Webster and Dr. Bob, however, it is clear that Webster was very mindful of letting Dr. Bob know which changes were being introduced, but it is not evident whether Webster had sent any proofs to Dr. Bob before the revised printings were published as he did with the first printing. Webster did, however, send copies of each new and revised printing. The following correspondence between Webster and both Dr. Bob and Bill W. provides a description of the reasons for the changes that Webster was incorporating into his book.[2]

The Correspondence between Webster and Dr. Bob

The development of Webster's ideas, and indeed his spirituality, which we shall discuss in Part Three, as presented in the early printings of the *Interpretation* finds a valuable backdrop in his exchange of letters with Dr. Bob prior to the latter's death in 1950.

On November 3, 1946, three months after the publication of the first printing, Dr. Bob wrote to Webster, thanking him for the book, which, in his laconic style he found to be "quite alright."

Webster replied on December 13, 1946, noting that on that very day, five years before, he had entered Alcoholics Anonymous, and he referred to it as a "Great Day." After relating what that day has meant to him, he provided an important reason for writing the book. Presenting the Twelve Steps to newcomers had always been his attempt to pay back in small measure what AA had done for him, and the appreciation of God's presence "was at the bottom of the Twelve Step Interpretation. The purpose was long-range sponsorship. It started in a small way with the boys in our group but has extended beyond that as a few other clubs seem to be using the little book as an outline for the study of the A.A. book. The demand is not great but the satisfaction is as I feel that others are getting a little help because of my cooperation with God, who saw fit to permit it."[3] The demand may not have been that great in the several months after the publication of the book, but it had a phenomenal increase in sales in subsequent years.

In reply Dr. Bob wrote that he "enjoyed your little book very much & know that it will prove to be of a lot of help to many."[4]

In the few years prior to his death, the correspondence between the two men shows that Dr. Bob became one of the strongest promoters of the book. Writing to Dr. Bob about the revisions in the second printing, Webster thanked him for recommending the book to Mr. Ritchey of Fort Lauderdale, who placed an order for fifty books. Webster made certain that Dr. Bob had a generous supply of books for those to whom he wished to give the *Interpretation*.

Webster also mentioned that the revisions in the second printing gave more complete coverage to the program. Formerly he overlooked commenting on drugs, spiritual blackouts, mental binges, mental blackouts, contemplated and attempted suicide, etc. These are included in the revised book as well as comments on serenity and a revision to the chapter on Fear, in Step Four.[5]

When Dr. Bob asked how much he owed for the revised copies, he was informed there was no charge for them. They were sent to Dr. Bob as a more complete interpretation of the program and were for his inspection and criticism. Any time Dr. Bob wanted more, he could simply ask. Once again Webster was grateful for the request from Fort Lauderdale as a "certain number have to be sold to keep the thing going. We do not quite break even, but it is a form of sponsorship, and finance is not a consideration so long as we do not see too much red."

He then went on to make a general comment on AA. "From all I hear about a lot of Southern Groups they need plenty of Interpretation. Many of them seem to take their A.A. too lightly. Barry and Don are busy with plans for the

Summer outing; there seems to be a lot of interest; hope it is a success. Will miss you and Anne."[6] It wasn't a success from a numbers standpoint. As noted before, the small attendance convinced Collins to abandon the retreats and some thought they were stopped "because it was not open to all and was thus against AA policy."[7]

A little over two years later, Webster wrote to Dr. Bob about another revision to the *Interpretation*, of which he had mailed him a few complimentary copies. "The book type has been raised from 10 to 12 points for easier reading. Some new matter added; some old dropped or changed." The letter also contained some new insights into Webster's spirituality:

> This habit of living consciously, daily with God, gives us strength for enduring that which has to be endured, energy for going ahead when the going is tough, insight into that which is and wisdom for planning the right way. Personally I have the Twelve Steps of AA to thank for recognition of the above fact and the degree of peace of mind and contented sobriety it has brought me. Your part in this is not overlooked. God and his agents share my appreciation.[8]

Toward the end of 1949, Dr. Bob was sick once again and a patient in St. Thomas Hospital. Webster and Collins had planned a trip to see him until they learned that he was in the hospital. Webster wrote about a fishing trip with Collins and John Harrington up the Temperance River. They found time to run up to Port Arthur, Canada, and spend the evening with the Thunder Bay group. Collins and Webster later returned to Port Arthur and spent two days and nights with them, giving lectures on the Twelve Steps. While there, visitors from the AA Assiniboine Group exacted a promise from them to repeat the meetings for them in Winnipeg.

Besides news about the Canadian outreach, Webster commented on the Nicollet group and the commitment required of its members. It had not grown rapidly, numbering about seventy-five, a natural consequence of the policies of the group. "Numerical values are not in our picture. We seek alcoholics who are earnestly desirous of gaining sobriety by making the Twelve Steps a Way of Life, will accept and live an orthodox interpretation of the Big Book. There is little drunkenness in our Fellowship and perhaps as much or more harmony than in most groups who have a Club Room and own considerable furnishing. It was good to have Bill with us several months ago; to have him one Sunday PM as our guest at open house. I say several months, it is really about a year ago. We miss you Bob and sincerely hope you can see us again when you feel better."[9]

Dr. Bob died in November 1950. His loss was deeply felt

by the members of the Nicollet group, as in their eyes he had assumed patriarchal stature.

Bill W.'s Early Involvement

Webster also kept Bill W. in the loop about the *Interpretation*, and although Bill had not gotten around to reading it, given the press of other problems, he wrote that others who have read it seem to like it very much.[10] Webster alerted Bill W. on the changes that were made in the revised edition:

> The introduction now reflects suggested usage of the book by AA groups and individuals. Usage that had been reported by many groups nationally and abroad. Numerous footnotes refer the reader to factual information in the book *Alcoholics Anonymous*. The word Disease has largely been replaced with Illness, Obsession, Sickness, etc. Wherever possible the word MUST has been removed. Correction to the proper mailing address of the WORKS PUBLISHING CO has been made and 60 other minor changes. . . If after you have read the revised copy you wish to make criticisms or corrections, please do so as they will be helpful in future revisions that we hope to make.[11]

This letter also reflects an increasingly broad market for the book. And as the market grew, so did Bill W.'s apprehension that the *Interpretation* would evolve into an accepted AA text for the Fellowship.

Webster shared with Bill how important the AA program was for him—"the most important thing in my life." His appreciation was best expressed by service, which he tried to render to alcoholics and others twenty-four hours a day. "I share part of this service in revision and distribution of the little red book. We have just completed a recent revision. . . Some new matter has been added, it can be found on pages Nos 8-24-34- and 111."

As they had with Dr. Bob, Webster reported on their outreach efforts to Port Arthur and Ft. Williams in Canada: "Funny about these new groups. It seems that someone has to explain that their answers are in the Big Book if they will but look for them. We left them with their noses in the Big Book. . . In our hearts Barry and I know that we have helped ourselves more than we could have possibly helped them."[12]

Bill W. visited Minneapolis in October 1948 and had the delicate and diplomatic task of giving equal time to both the Alano and Nicollet Clubs. It was a balancing act that both Bill W. and the New York office often engaged in. Invitations to visit Minneapolis and the distribution of inquiries about AA from that area had to include both clubs. Some months after this visit, Bill W. wrote to Webster: "Lois and I continue to reminisce about our pleasant visit with your group. God forbid that Alcoholics Anonymous ever become frozen or rigid in its way of doing or thinking. Within the framework of our principles the ways are apparently legion. There is little doubt that the contribution you folks have made to our progress will always be a part of the folk lore of our well-loved fellowship." [13]

Webster's Strict Interpretation of the Big Book

In the introduction to the *Interpretation,* Webster provides a list of reasons why certain drinkers do not succeed in their recovery. In the 1946 printing the seventh reason reads: "The alcoholic who is 'constitutionally dishonest' has *no* chance. He cannot be honest with himself." The 1949 printing reads: "The alcoholic who is 'constitutionally dishonest' has *little* chance. He cannot be honest with himself." Webster's earliest thinking, which supported his "no chance" attitude, can be found in the annotation in Webster's Big Book (second edition). In Chapter Five, "How It Works," the first sentence reads: "Rarely have we seen a person fail who has thoroughly followed our path." In the upper margin there is an arrow pointing to the word "rarely" for which Webster has printed in large bold letters the word "Never."

Another example of Webster's "strict interpretation" revolves about the word "must." Someone may have brought to Webster's attention that his frequent use of the word "must" might weigh too heavily on readers new to the program, particularly in view of what Bill W. wrote commenting on the First Tradition: "Alcoholics Anonymous has no musts . . . We do suggest but we don't discipline."[14] Webster wrote to Bill W., "Where ever possible the word 'must' has been removed."[15] Compare page 19 of the 1946 printing, where each of the twelve important considerations for recovery contains the word "must," with page 23 of the 1949 printing; not one of the considerations includes the word. Webster's thinking, as revealed in his writings, testifies in its own way to the strong demands put upon those seeking membership in the Nicollet group in order to prevent "slips." Webster proceeded to encapsulate in dark red lines (sometimes blue) the word "must" wherever found in his Big Book to prove that the word needed to be taken seriously as an integral part of the whole program. In later editions of *The Little Red Book,* thirty-four of these "musts" found in the Big Book are included in an appendix entitled, "We Don't Have To But." The explanation for the inclusion: "Living the Twelve Steps was not compulsory, yet as we grew in understanding of our new way of life, we realized that it embraced many voluntary 'musts.'"

—

Stage II: 1950–1967

The relationship between Webster and Bill W. regarding both *The Little Red Book* and *Twelve Steps and Twelve Traditions* plays a significant role during this period.

Bill W.'s Changing Views on *The Little Red Book*

On October 28, 1946, shortly after the *Interpretation* was first officially published in August of that year, Webster sent a copy to Bill W. In response Bill W. wrote:

> The press of priority problems has been so great I haven't had a chance to get at the little book. Everybody who has read it seems to like it very much—which of course is to be expected!
>
> Personally I am very glad to see many people writing about A.A. and circulating the material about it even though some folks seem to think I should do all the writing. To me this idea is nonsense. A.A. is not one point of view, it is many. When writing I do not ["not"

is crossed out] always try to be a mirror for what seems to be the majority opinion.

My feeling about material sent out to the group list is as follows: If the stuff is good it will be used and will be helpful; if no good it will be thrown in the wastebasket [sic]. It is almost as simple as that despite our "viewers with alarm."[1]

As will be seen, this letter stood in strong contrast with the views that he later expressed to others regarding the *Interpretation* (and later *The Little Red Book)* and about the need for a committee of the Board to determine what would be accepted into the corpus of approved AA literature.

Over a month after Bill W.'s visit to Minneapolis two years later in October 1948, he was beginning to show some concern about the proliferation of AA literature:

I feel that any A.A. or interested person, ought to be able to write anything at all about us and the general problem. . . Also some of us are beginning to feel that there should be such a thing as standard A.A. literature. Meaning, of course, a traditional right of our general headquarters to issue standard texts on the A.A. program and its ramifications. Your volume would not, of course, fall into this category at all.[2]

In the early years after the publication of the *Interpretation*, Bill W. appeared to have welcomed the book and to have had a warm relationship with both Ed Webster and Barry Collins, appreciative of the good work that they were doing. As late as 1950, Bill W. wrote to Collins, "*The Little Red Book* does fill a definite need and has wide circulation. Therefore its usefulness is unquestioned." The ideas for *Twelve Steps and Twelve Traditions* were already percolating in his mind: "Someday I may try to write an introduction book myself which I hope might complement favorably with *The Little Red Book*. Here at the Foundation we are not policemen; we're a service and AAs are free to read any book they choose."[3]

But Bill W.'s concern about *The Little Red Book* had already been growing. Eight months earlier, he had written to Clem L.:

> While the tract like the Minneapolis book has proved rather popular and useful, I do think it sets a rather bad precedent. It is frankly a textbook, seemingly endorsed by Dr. Bob and me, and it is distributed through A.A. channels. As our membership grows so will the temptation to go into the A.A. textbook business with or without our approval. That could lead to hopeless confusion and recrimination. I suppose the best answer would be for me to

write better textbooks. People seem to expect that I will, and I hope that one day I shall find the wit and time to do that.[4]

As the popularity of *The Little Red Book* continued to grow, taking on the role of a Twelve Step textbook, Bill W.'s correspondence began to show further signs of concern. He wrote: "Since drunks talk freely, why should they not write freely? To this inclusive concept, I can think of only one desirable exception. I question whether any A.A. group or individual, unless directly authorized by the Foundation, ought to issue anything which could be regarded as a standard A.A. textbook. To that extent and that extent only, do I think that the A.A. movement ought to control its own literature. . ."[5]

Then, shortly before Dr. Bob died, Bill W. wrote that the situation on *The Little Red Book* is "a little bit delicate." He continued:

The Red Book does fill a definite need, and has pretty wide circulation, several thousand copies a year. Therefore, its usefulness is unquestioned. A.A. has a definite place for such a book.

But its publication, as a standard textbook by two individual AAs in a private enterprise does raise certain questions for the future.

QUESTIONS of precedent. Someday, I suppose, A.A. will have to define what standard textbooks are and probably reserve the right to prepare and publish them to the Foundation or its nominees. Otherwise, the widened book market which our continued growth will certainly bring will present a temptation to many ambitious members to enter the textbook field with their own individual ideas. Over the years, if the Red Book precedent stands, it could well happen, creating a chaotic state in our basic literature.

. . . I am not inclined to make an issue at this point.

Someday I may try to write an introductory book myself which I hope might compete favorably with the Red Book. At that time we could ask A.A. as a whole (through the General Service Conference to be formed) to inaugurate a Tradition covering the longer future.[6]

Shortly after the death of Dr. Bob, Ed Webster wrote to Bill W., commenting on the important role Dr. Bob had played for the past fifteen years and informing Bill W. that he has "mailed out about 450 complimentary copies (latest revision) along with the same letter (bulletin 13?) you will receive. Some of these books have gone to groups we are dealing with and others to groups who have not heard about the book before."[7]

Two days later, unaware of Bill W.'s ambivalence, Webster wrote to him again:

> . . . This letter (Bulletin?). . . was sent, numbered about 800 in all. I imagine we will probably get a reprimand from the Foundation Office as we did in February of this year, but if so they will be wrong in assuming we are using the AA Directory. Our many traveling members have supplied us with the names of secretaries, PO Box numbers. This information combined with our own communications with groups and individuals has allowed us to compile a list of perhaps 900 names and PO Boxes. Our letters have gone to groups or people on this list.[8]

The use of the AA directory as a mailing list for *The Little Red Book* or *Bulletin 13* became another point of contention between New York and Nicollet. The focus for Nicollet was "carrying the message." The focus for Bill W. was the issue of the "unauthorized textbook" and the New York "mailing lists."

A short time later, Webster followed up with another

letter in which he wrote that "carrying the message is the purpose of the little book. It is our sponsorship endeavor and that we give away about 10 per cent of our publication in this manner."[9] As I've noted, sponsorship, either personally or through the gift of *The Little Red Book*, played a very important role in the Nicollet group.

Toward the end of the same month, Bill W. again brought up the textbook issue with another person:

> But I don't believe individual AAs ought to get into the text book business. In this respect, it is probable the Minneapolis Red Book has gone over far. It is, in fact, what purports to be a standard AA text. Actually, it reflects the ideas of a single group or area, and is the private property, I believe of individuals. Because it is a useful volume, filling a distinct place, and we have never offered anything better from down here, I have been loathe to raise this question. In fact, it isn't my place to raise it. It is a matter for movement representatives to decide. But you can readily see that if this precedent stands, any AA member or group could enter the standard textbook business and so hopelessly confuse our literature situation over a period of years.[10]

Indeed *The Little Red Book* reflected more than the mind of a single group. It reflected also the ideas of Dr. Bob, the cofounder of Alcoholics Anonymous. It would seem that Bill W. did tread lightly while Dr. Bob was alive. After Dr. Bob died on November 17, 1950, however, Bill W. conveyed his feelings about the issue more openly. It would be wrong to portray Dr. Bob's approach to AA as representative of a single group. Rather, like Bill W., he spoke for the whole of AA, even though his roots were in the Midwest. Bill W. was also representative of the whole of AA, even though his roots and early influence were grounded in the East Coast. Dr. Bob was a big booster of *The Little Red Book*, and as such provided a wider audience than just Minneapolis. He insisted that New York have copies of it in the warehouse for a wider distribution. His correspondence testifies to how highly he recommended it. With his passing Webster (and, indeed, the Nicollet Club) lost a dear friend and a strong supporter of their book.

The year 1950 was important also for the circulation of Bill W.'s idea for a General Service Conference, representing all of AA and responsible for its unity and service. The increasing number of tracts that professed to be speaking for AA, which included *The Little Red Book* and the recognition it was receiving, prompted the General Service Conference to adopt the concept of conference-approved literature in 1951, to be overseen by a trustee's literature committee. They in turn would propose what the conference should accept as "true" or basic AA literature.[11]

On February 15, 1952, Webster, unaware of Bill W.'s increasingly negative reaction to the role *The Little Red Book* was playing in AA circles, wrote to him, forwarding copies of the 1952 printing. Among the revisions that he made, he felt that the one reworking the Third Step was important. Essentially it promoted the idea that we know that we have made a decision to turn our will and lives over to God as we understand Him when we are living and practicing Steps Four through Twelve. Webster ended the letter with an example of how the Nicollet group was practicing the Twelfth Step. They had forwarded one hundred copies of *The Little Red Book* as a gift to a London AA group. He considered it an example of Nicollet's practice of long-range sponsorship. He ended the letter by writing: "I'll bet they will be surprised upon receiving them."[12]

It is not clear whether Bill W. was pleased with Nicollet's Twelfth Step outreach efforts or considered it another example of a local group speaking for the whole of AA. However, some months later Bill W. had a surprise for Webster. He wrote to him outlining the writings in which he was engaged and his plans for the future:

"I'm also working on a small book, now three fourths completed, which will consist of twelve pieces on the A.A. Traditions, now currently running in the Grapevine, and twelve pieces of about 2,000 words each on the Twelve Steps. None of these attempted essays will go very far into actual application. They are more intended and deepen the under- standing of both Steps and Traditions." Bill W. continued, outlining future writing projects on the Twelve Steps and their wider application to other problems, as well as a short history of AA: "So that the main facts can be set straight and so that the average member can see how the Steps, Traditions and Services evolve." [13]

The letter obviously took Webster by surprise. The im- minent publication of *Twelve Steps and Twelve Traditions* in 1952 led to all sorts of questions and feelings on the part of Webster and other members of the Nicollet Club. *The Little Red Book* had an ever-widening circulation and for many it was the best interpretation of the Twelve Steps even though it was not the official one. Webster and his group did not want to give the appearance of being in competition with one of the founders of AA. And Dr. Bob, who had not been a great advocate of the Twelve Traditions, was no longer there to support the Nicollet group. For some years he had been at odds with Bill W. about the need for the Traditions and subsequently about the idea of the General Service Conference composed of representatives of the Fellowship. It was not until 1950 and his last appearance at the First International Convention at Cleveland that "he agreed to confirm the Twelve Traditions," as well as extending his support of the General Service Conference.[14]

Upon receiving Bill W.'s letter, Webster wrote that the Nicollet Club at first believed that the route to take was to discontinue *The Little Red Book* except for local sponsorship use. However, AA members from a wide geographical range objected on the grounds that their groups needed *The Little Red Book*. After much prayerful consideration, the decision was made to continue the circulation of the book. A twenty-five cent increase per copy would be sent to the New York Office of AA. It was decided also that on January 1, 1964, they would cease all publication of the book and turn the copyright of the book over to AA New York.[15] Instead the copyright was sold to the Hazelden Foundation in 1967. Over the years, it was only natural that each book would find a coterie of supporters who would advance reasons in support of one over the other, or indeed support of both. By 1964, *The Little Red Book* had been translated into eight languages, including versions for all of the Scandinavian countries, French, German, Italian, and Spanish. Even after *Twelve Steps and Twelve Traditions* was published, *The Little Red Book* continued to be used in groups where it was felt that the latter was a more practical introduction to the Twelve Steps than the more philosophical material in Bill W.'s book.

Expansion of *The Little Red Book* and
Other Writings by Webster

Over the course of the subsequent printings of *The Little Red Book,* the topic that emerges most strongly in Webster's thinking is the Twelfth Step and "carrying the message." In the 1953 printing of the volume, there is a long appendix containing a further explanation of the mechanics of working the Twelfth Step. It is called "Working with Others," and contains questions and answers on sponsorship with, as usual, references to the Big Book. Essential to "carrying the message" was seeing that *The Little Red Book* was available to others, either through sales or by gift, as we have seen above in the case of the 100 copies that were sent free of charge to an AA group in England.

In the second appendix of the 1953 revision, Webster decides to list all those places in the Big Book where the word "must" has been used. Apparently this was to demonstrate to his critics that his previous use of the word "must" was validated in and by the Big Book. In this same printing, Webster elaborates further on the meaning of surrender: "We come to know God (and surrender to Him) from living the Twelve Steps."

The 1957 printing featured the identification of subjects in the first and second editions of the Big Book with single references. More importantly Webster enlarged the book by eight pages, including a report on opinions, national and international, relative to the importance of a spiritual awakening. He also included in the Step Twelve chapter suggestions for a specific outline for the working mechanics of sponsorship and eliminated the appendices "Working with Others," "Questions and Answers," and "We Don't Have To But. . ." The 1960–61 printings resurrected these latter two appendices, but continued the inclusion of "Working with Others" in the chapter on the Twelfth Step.

Stools and Bottles

During this period, Webster's literary output was not limited to revisions of *The Little Red Book*, the most popular and successful of his writings. He added two other volumes that attracted many of the same readers. One of these, *Stools and Bottles*, finds its logical, if not chronological, place here.

Webster described the little volume, which was first published in 1955, as an "illustrated book designed for the beginner and for old timers showing signs of complacency." By visual aids, it depicts the seat of a legless stool, comparing it with the newcomer seeking recovery—off balance, helpless, and incomplete until AA provides legs of support. In the book, the first three Steps are each a leg of a three-legged stool—each one an essential part if the stool is to be sat upon without wobbling or crashing. Eight empty whiskey bottles are used to illustrate the character defects, which need to be dealt with in Step Four.

Webster gives his popular "Stools and Bottles" talk, circa 1955.

Webster ends the book with thirty-one brief meditations for each day of the month. They bear a resemblance to Richmond Walker's *Twenty-Four Hours a Day*, which provides a Thought for the Day, a Meditation, and a Prayer for the Day. Similarly, Webster spells out a "Reminder," a "Daily Inventory," a "Suggested Meditation," a "Spiritual Contact," and a "Daily Physical Audit." The latter is intended to "point out the physical pitfalls and mental barriers which obstruct recovery in AA." In Part Three on Webster's ideas on spirituality, we shall scrutinize his chapter on the Third Step to reflect on his important and evolving insights on "turning over one's will."

Bar Room Reveries and *Our Devilish Alcoholic Personalities*

Three years later, in 1958, Webster published *Bar Room Reveries*. He himself considered it a humorous book with close to three hundred "drinking jokes, puns, anecdotes and a few amusing, true drinking experiences." Webster considered it a uniquely different book from which speakers could draw to inject some humor into their talks when it seemed appropriate. Readers fortunate to come across a copy (only a thousand were printed) can judge for themselves how the humor holds up. Today the value of the book is not so much in its contents as in its rarity. It adds hardly anything to our understanding and knowledge of Webster's evolving spirituality, except that he had a sense of humor and understood its important place both in keeping us human and in the alcoholic's recovery.

In 1970, Webster published his final work, *Our Devilish Alcoholic Personalities*. This little volume, perhaps the least known of Webster's works, expresses in a special way the struggle between the two selves in each of us. In the case of recovery, the Alcoholic Personality stands in sharp contrast to the Recovering Personality, upon which recovery is grounded. We shall give special attention to this work in a later chapter.

Stage III: Hazelden and *The Little Red Book*

1967 AND AFTER

In 1952, the Butlers, a very prominent and successful mining family, purchased Hazelden, a fledgling treatment center north of Minnesota's Twin Cities. Patrick Butler, who became president of Hazelden, was responsible for the center's early growth and stability. In recovery himself, Butler sensed that the field was on the edge of a new frontier. He was determined to assist alcoholics by associating the Minnesota Model, espoused by Hazelden, with the seminal scientific research conducted at Yale through the Yale Summer School of Alcohol Studies. (The school later moved to Rutgers, where Dan Anderson, who succeeded Butler as the president of Hazelden, would lecture for many years on the multidisciplinary approach to the treatment of alcoholism.)

Under Butler's leadership, the publication and marketing of writings about recovery became an important part of the Hazelden mission. The seeds of Hazelden's publishing mission were sown in 1952, when Butler came across a small volume titled *Twenty-Four Hours a Day,* the first meditation book written expressly for recovering alcoholics. The author, Richmond Walker, was publishing, selling, and distributing the volume himself from his home in Daytona Beach, Florida. Butler thought so highly of the little book and what it might mean to all recovering alcoholics that two years later in February 1954, he offered to publish and distribute the work. Walker accepted Butler's offer after the General Service Board of Alcoholics Anonymous showed no interest in the undertaking. In May 1954, Hazelden purchased the rights to *Twenty-Four Hours a Day.*[1]

By 2012, the book had sold more than 10 million copies and remains to this day one of Hazelden's best sellers. It is curious to note that early in May 1954, Ed Webster had contacted Richmond Walker to ask if he wished to sell his book to Coll-Web, Webster's own publishing company. Webster seemed unaware that Butler had asked about purchasing the rights to *Twenty-Four Hours a Day* three months earlier.

Both Pat Butler, president of Hazelden, and Dan Anderson, its vice president and director, recognized the value and inspirational nature of *The Little Red Book.* Ever since his purchase of *Twenty-Four Hours a Day,* Butler continued to watch for literature that would enrich the spirituality of the recovering alcoholic and enhance Hazelden in the public eye. On June 28, 1967, Hazelden purchased the rights to *The Little Red Book* from Ed Webster and his wife,

Hazel, along with 20,000 copies of *The Little Red Book* and *Stools and Bottles* that Webster had stored in his basement. The purchase price was $1.25 per copy. Hazelden also agreed to hire Webster as a consultant for the preparation and sale of subsequent editions of the book. The agreement stipulated that Webster would lecture once a month at Hazelden headquarters in Center City, Minnesota. He was to be paid $200 per month for his services as consultant and lecturer. If Webster were to die, his wife would receive the benefit of $200 without having to lecture.[2]

After this initial agreement between Webster and Butler, which lasted for three years, the relationship got a little rocky. In 1970, when Hazelden undertook another printing of the book under its own copyright, Webster was granted royalties for a ten-year period. For some reason, Hazelden neglected to follow through on the royalty payments, and Webster reminded Hazelden five months later in April 1971 of its failure to abide by their mutual agreement. "I am asking that you rectify this situation as promptly as possible by giving me a royalty contract without delay."[3] On June 3, 1971, shortly after the contract was signed, Webster died at the age of seventy-nine.

Bill Pittman's Role

During this third period in the history of *The Little Red Book*, Bill Pittman, who was involved in the collection and establishment of the Hazelden-Pittman Archives, played a pivotal role. Pittman's research and writings on the origins and early history of Alcoholics Anonymous are also important.[4]

Because of his interest in and love of history, Butler was also aware of the importance of books and papers referencing the history of alcoholism and recovery. In Bill Pittman, he discovered the person who could build a collection at Hazelden, a collection that became well respected among archivists and historians in the field of alcoholism throughout the United States.

After graduating from the University of Minnesota, Pittman received an academic internship at the AA office in New York, where he worked at the *Grapevine* office, and began graduate studies at New York University. From his new East Coast location, Pittman was able to rummage through the bookshops in New York, adding to his collections of temperance, Prohibition, and AA material, which he sent to Hazelden for storage. This rich vein of historical material became the basis for the Hazelden-Pittman Archives, which were inaugurated in 1993 at Hazelden in a ceremony attended by AA archivists, historians, and scholars from throughout the United States.[5]

When Pittman officially assumed his position as director of the archives in 1994, one of the first projects to gain his attention was *The Little Red Book*, which had a fiftieth anniversary coming up in 1996. Hazelden had published another printing in 1970, with a revised edition under Hazelden's copyright following in 1986. (This latter attempt to improve upon Webster's style did not appeal to some of the old-timers, who believed the changes were unwarranted and of dubious value.) Pittman believed *The Little Red Book* was one of the most important spiritual books of early AA history. He dedicated much time and effort to gathering various editions as well as material on its historical background, including information on the Nicollet Club, Ed Webster, Barry Collins, and Dr. Bob.

Pittman wrote a valuable foreword to the anniversary edition, based on resources he had collected over the years, some of which remain unpublished. But for some reason he made a very egregious error. Instead of using the 1946 and first printing (Roman numeral MCMXLVI) of the book as the source for the fiftieth anniversary edition, he published the 1949 printing (Roman numeral MCMXLIX). By the time this unfortunate error was brought to his attention, it was too late to do anything since the volume had already gone to press and was being distributed. Both editor and publisher were embarrassed that retailers and buyers were getting the forty-seventh anniversary edition instead of the fiftieth. What was done could not be undone.

Despite his mistake and the embarrassment that accompanied it, Pittman continued to show a special interest in *The Little Red Book,* collecting as many printings as he could find.[6] In 1998, he published *The Little Red Book Study Guide*, designed to meet the needs of both AA study groups and of newcomers to AA who were working the program on their own. The book was intended to provide the structure needed to live the Twelve Steps.

PART III

Spirituality in
The Little Red Book

Spirituality was a lifelong experience for Webster.

Is there really something "spiritual" about the whole process of addiction and recovery? *The Little Red Book* responds with a resounding yes. The reason *The Little Red Book* became so popular in the AA community was that it described spirituality in very specific and concrete terms—the transition from the alcoholic personality to the recovering personality. AA also captures what is essential to spirituality—the recognition that "our journey through life is a community affair—someone has to say 'I will be with you.'"

■ ■ ■

Reflections on Spirituality

Since the word "spirituality" appears often on the following pages, it makes sense to pause at this point and reflect on what is meant by the term. I do not consider myself an expert in this matter, but I do bring to the discussion two experiences. The first is what I have seen over the past thirty years in my own personal life as a Franciscan priest. The second is my work at Hazelden for the same length of time, where I have encountered the Twelve Steps and witnessed firsthand how spirituality has entered and affected the lives of the patients. I dealt with my experiences of spirituality with Hazelden at great length in my book, *The Essence of Twelve Step Recovery*, upon which this chapter relies. In it I suggested that all spirituality is *relational* and that the Twelve Step program is a quintessential example of this *relational spirituality*. Likewise, *The Little Red Book* argues strongly in favor of that thesis. For example, in his interpretation of the Fourth Step, Webster emphasized this point: The object of the Step is to bring about thorough honesty—"Honesty with yourself, God, and with your fellowman."[1]

My introduction to what I call relational spirituality

came in my experiences as a Franciscan. When I was first introduced to the Franciscan way of life, I was captivated by the strength and sense of community it exhibited. I must admit that their brown robes, cords, and cowls the members wore were quite distinctive and set them apart. But it was their camaraderie and care for one another that really attracted me. I knew nothing about the vows they had taken or their prayer life. It was the fraternity (fellowship) and their caring for one another that spilled over into the care for the poor, both material and spiritual, that I found compelling. The person who inspired these men to embrace such a life was Francis of Assisi, called the *Poverello*—"the Little Poor Man," who lived eight and half centuries ago. His life and voice continue to inspire today, as it did most recently when the present Pope of the Catholic Church took his new name after Francis of Assisi.

But there was more to being a Franciscan than just the fellowship. I had to learn about the demands this life would put upon me personally. The admission ceremony to the novitiate (a year of testing and learning what the Franciscan life was all about) consisted of clothing me with the Franciscan habit (robe), which symbolized my putting aside the "old" man and putting on the "new" man. The vows of poverty, chastity, and obedience that we took were intended to replace our self-centeredness and direct us toward a God-centered world. To help us grow in this "other centeredness," we were taught the tools of spiritual reading, prayer, meditation, and all sorts of spiritual exercises to keep the old man in check and allow the new man to flourish. Daily attendance, followed by daily celebration of the Eucharist as a priest, created a formidable spiritual arsenal to accompany, guide, and protect us on our journey. It was a new way of life, and the spiritual tools that we were given had to be exercised on a daily basis. In other words "the spiritual life was not just a theory," it had to be lived—and lived through the practice of the vows of poverty, chastity, and obedience. The goal was to be as perfect as our Heavenly Father was perfect. (Later, "Progress not perfection" became a much more realistic and attainable goal.)

I was a model Franciscan for two decades, but then the events of Vatican II and the changes it implemented struck with unexpected force. The Catholic Church seemed to go into a tailspin. No one was exempt from the turmoil and upset that spread through all levels and corners of the Church. I was given a series of assignments that took their toll on me both spiritually and psychologically. The external claims upon my talents and time drew me further and further away from the life I had professed.

In autumn 1976, I came to Minnesota to participate in the Hazelden Center City treatment facility's Clinical Pastoral Education Program. It was the best year of my life and the worst year of my life. It was during that time that

I was invited to look into myself, and with that new self-knowledge and self-understanding, I would be able to better help patients. But it was a torturous year for me. I had fallen in love and was wearing the masks of Jekyll and Hyde, pretending to be and accepted as this gifted pastoral and celibate counselor while at the same time professing love and promising marriage to someone who thought I was honest about my intentions.

Failing to live the celibate life that I had vowed and unwilling to lead a double life, I made the decision to leave the priesthood and the Franciscan order. I decided to end a way of life that I had embraced for some thirty years. My spiritual life was sterile and empty. After a brief return to the Franciscans, I made the decision to return to Hazelden, where I would remain for the next thirty years. After rising in the ranks to the position of executive vice president, I returned to the position that I had started out with—working with patients as a chaplain for the next fifteen years. That, and my marriage to a patient and loving woman, has enriched my life and provided the foundation for developing my talents in public speaking and lecturing to the patients every week on the Twelve Steps. Like Ed Webster, I made a point of studying the Twelve Steps very carefully before lectures, preparing myself to present the meaning of the Steps, the gift of relational spirituality that Bill W. had bequeathed to the AA community. During that time, my two constant companions were *Twenty-Four Hours a Day* and *The Little Red Book*. From reading and lecturing over the years, I came to a fuller but still open-ended understanding of the nature of spirituality that is laid before us in the Twelve Steps and their interpretation in *The Little Red Book*.

What, then, is behind what I call the relational spirituality as exemplified in *The Little Red Book*? What does it mean to be a spiritual person?

Too often in our modern society, the word spirituality serves as a catchall for a sanitized, feel-good, boutique, therapeutic "something" that makes no demands, calls for no sacrifice, asks for no conversion, but only soothes and affirms. It is a "glow word," defying definition except that its use makes us feel better. It is simply more popular among many people to be spiritual and rather old-fashioned to be religious. These understandings or misunderstandings (conceptions or misconceptions) of spirituality are the reasons why it is so difficult to engage in a disciplined discussion or even the *practice* of spirituality.

Over the course of seventy years, I have had two careers. As a Franciscan priest, my spirituality and religious practices derived from the great commandment of Love—God, neighbor, and self. Then in the second half of life, during my thirty years at Hazelden, I was no longer a member of a religious order but I discovered the spirituality of AA, which had as its center the Twelve Steps. Around these Steps orbited relationships with the God of one's understanding, with others, and with one's real self. Looking back over both stages of my life, it reinforced my evolving conviction that *all spirituality is relational.* It wasn't a onetime experience, but rather a gradual awakening as my life continues to unfold.

That all spirituality is relational makes it so much easier to understand and practice what is written in *The Big Book of Alcoholics Anonymous:* "The spiritual life is not a theory. We have to live it."[2] One of the most fundamental yearnings of human nature is to be connected to other human beings, and through them to the God of our understanding—in other words, to be relational. Herein also lies the essentials of the spirituality of recovery as contained in the Twelve Steps, a thesis explained and elaborated upon by Webster in *The Little Red Book.*

Given this understanding of spirituality, one of the most insidious aspects of alcoholism and addiction to other drugs and behaviors such as gambling is that it is anti-relational. In his seminal book *The Addictive Personality,* Craig Nakken describes addiction as a pathological relationship of love and trust with an object or event other than with the true self, with others, and with a God of their understanding. It is a downward, twisting, tornado-like funnel that tosses aside, like so much debris, relationships with self, spouse, children, parents, friends, and the God of their understanding or their Higher Power. It makes shambles of our lives. Our journey through life is meant to be a community affair in which someone has committed to say, "I will be with you."

As part of this downward spiral, the alcoholic personality compels us against our will to substitute that which is most important to us as human beings—intimacy/closeness with another/others—for our relationship with alcohol or other mood-altering substances and behaviors. As Nakken writes, there is a terrible disconnect from reality. Over the course of the alcoholic journey, the individual moves from the land of the living to the land of objects. No matter how hard one tries, one cannot have intimacy with an object. It is difficult to breathe (spirit = breath) when one's spirit is being crushed from within.

With the loss of relationships there emerges a full-blown negative value system described in the Big Book as one composed of self-centeredness, fear, dishonesty, and resentment. These heighten the formidable barriers to the relationships that are the warp and woof of what makes us human.

"The bottom of the spiral is a place, sacred or unholy, where one loathes being, where one experiences a personal hell with all its demons," this author noted in *The Essence of Twelve Step Recovery*. "This disconnectedness and feeling of 'relational abandonment' becomes so complete, the pain so unrelenting, the hopelessness so unremitting, that the alcoholic feels that he is dying. He will do anything to lessen the pain, push back the tide of despair, relieve the loneliness and hopelessness, and absolve himself of the shame and guilt. More alcohol provides only a momentary relief. The loss of the spirit is so pronounced that suddenly there is the whisper from our demons that this life is no longer worth living."[3] In the vast majority of cases alcoholics are never totally abandoned, as Webster himself discovered. The potential for recovery is always there. Certainly the God of one's understanding will not abandon the individual. No matter how hopeless the situation may seem to the alcoholic, family members and friends will usually continue to manifest and extend their love. This was the case with Ed Webster, whose wife, Marian, contacted the nascent AA group guided by Pat Cronin. In other instances an alcoholic may stumble upon someone who is in the Fellowship, or a member of that community may be led to seek out the alcoholic.

When alcoholics discover that their own strength and efforts have been to no avail, they may have another discovery: that the strength of others is sufficient. Trusting in that strength, the addict begins to heal/mend through the relationship and redemptive power of others, reflecting the slow but certain recognition of a Higher Power in the collective strength of a community whose members have gone through similar descending/ascending journeys.

Real transformation occurs with the hand of the helpless one reaching out to grasp the hand of the helper—the beginning of the spiritual awakening. Finally, it is the humble acknowledgement that "I cannot do it by myself; I need others to help me." This leads to the gradual recovery of one's lost "relational" spirituality. It is the principles of this relational spirituality, this "new way of life" that Ed Webster has taught thousands of recovering alcoholics in *The Little Red Book*.

Clearly the Steps, relational in character, are meant to restore relationships with self, with others, and with the God of our understanding. In the following diagram I have sorted the Steps into circles and arranged them into three groups. Circles represent continuity, protection, strength, and completeness, and they seemed an appropriate way to express our relationship with self, others, and a Higher Power. The Steps divide themselves comfortably into three distinct triads intended to cultivate and strengthen these relationships[4] (see next page).

These Steps allow us to recover the normal relationship/ intimacy with our real selves, with others (family, friends), and with the God of our understanding. All of the Steps are involved in healing these relationships. Where disintegration prevailed, integrity assumes the commanding role.

Refreshing in its simplicity, Webster's spirituality is based entirely upon the Twelve Steps discussed in *The Little Red Book*. It rests on the fundamental principle of self-knowledge resulting in a personality change that allows one to lead a sober life. For the tension between the "old man" and the "new man," he substitutes the interplay between the

The Twelve Steps

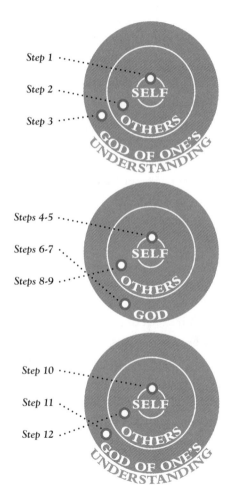

Step 1

Step 2

Step 3

SELF

OTHERS

GOD OF ONE'S UNDERSTANDING

Steps 4-5

Steps 6-7

Steps 8-9

SELF

OTHERS

GOD

Step 10

Step 11

Step 12

SELF

OTHERS

GOD OF ONE'S UNDERSTANDING

The quality of our relationship with the God of our understanding is absolutely contingent upon the quality of our own relationship with others.

alcoholic personality and the recovering personality. In his explanation of the Twelve Steps he chooses as his theme the idea of a "personality change" found in appendix II of the Big Book. To make his point, he sets up a dialectic between the "alcoholic" personality and the "recovering" personality and demonstrates how the former will surrender to the latter in the understanding and practice of each of the Steps. Webster saw growth in the spiritual life as the outcome of this struggle. Webster's most striking description of the struggle can be found in *Our Devilish Alcoholic Personalities,* written the year before he died.

This duality and the struggle contained therein are mirrored in the history of Western thought. The following are but a few selections.

Carl Jung said it best when he commented, "What drives people to war with themselves is the intuition or knowledge that they consist of two people in opposition to one another. The conflict may be between the sensual and spiritual man, or between the ego and the shadow. It is what Faust means when he says: 'Two souls, alas, dwell within my breast apart.'"[5]

Almost two millennia previously, the great Christian missionary Paul of Tarsus testified to the same truth when he wrote, "I do not do what I want to—and what I do I detest. Miserable man that I am! Who will save me from the body of this death?" (Romans 7:24) Both of these men testify clearly and strongly to their belief that there is another self within us waiting to snare us, to exploit, control, and distort each of our lives.

The following story has been passed on in a variety of ways. It goes something like this: We all have two dogs inside of us. One is a junkyard dog that is always barking and yapping, clawing, and straining at anyone or anything moving. The other is a Prince Charles spaniel that is just waiting to greet us at the front door. It is always friendly and just wants to jump on our laps and be petted. It is human nature, says the storyteller: we all have both dogs inside us. When the storyteller is asked which dog wins, he smiles and responds, "Whichever dog you are feeding."

In the following chapter we will see how Webster explored the emergence of the new recovering person in each of the Steps and the qualities that define recovery. Then, in the final chapter, we will explore the concept and reality of "surrender" and the relationship between our will and God's will in the matter of recovery.

The Idea of Personality Change
in *The Little Red Book*

The idea of a personality change in recovery is highlighted in appendix II of the Big Book, as follows: "The terms 'spiritual experience' and 'spiritual awakening' are used many times in this book which, upon careful reading, shows that the personality change sufficient to bring about recovery from alcoholism has manifested itself among us in many forms." This personality change is not ordinarily in the form of a "sudden or spectacular upheaval," or "an immediate and overwhelming 'God consciousness' followed at once by a vast change in feeling and outlook." These personality changes are mostly of "the 'educational variety' because they develop slowly over a period of time." The principles that fashion the personality change are the Twelve Steps of Alcoholics Anonymous; they are also described in the commentary in *The Little Red Book*.

The Big Book was sacred to Ed Webster. With some trepidation and remaining faithful to Bill W.'s text, he wrote the various editions of his book as a *commentary* on the Twelve Steps, to show the path to this new personality.

In the margins of his personal copy of *The Interpretation of the Twelve Steps of Alcoholics Anonymous* (the second printing, 1947), Webster scribbled some additional commentary on his own text. In a sense these can be described as spontaneous meditations that Webster shared with the audience while commenting on the Steps. These latter annotations provide some of the best insights into his spirituality. Written a little more than a decade after the founding of AA and a little more than seven years after the Big Book was published, both the text and the marginal annotations capture the willingness to go to any lengths to reinstate one's real personality through the gift of sobriety.

Added to these two major sources is a third: *Our Devilish Alcoholic Personalities*, which Webster wrote the year before he died and referred to with the playful acronym ODAP. In this little volume he describes in vivid and realistic detail what any alcoholic can relate to—how the alcoholic personality subtly seeks to reinstate itself into the mind and soul of the recovering person by sabotaging the ongoing recovery process. Indeed, it resonates with the heart and mind of every alcoholic on the road to recovery. "So it came to pass that a hostile little MENTAL MONKEY named ODAP subtly invaded the ranks of AA where he still clings to the shoulders of its members whispering harmful anti-sober temptations into their ears."[1] This is something akin to the "monkey mind," a Buddhist concept described as a self-criticizing aspect of our mind that swings us from doubt to worry and back to doubt. "Monkey mind chatters the most loudly when we threaten to change the status quo."[2]

He ends this essay with an important reflection: "For the purpose of identification and comparison, I have used the analogy of two opposite powers in the A.A. Fellowship to emphasize the help of a Higher Power, and the barriers which ODAP builds up to obstruct our efforts to live a normal, sober life."[3] Webster's book describes his own personal experiences with "this detestable little ape" as he continued to work the program over the years since his recovery. "Even so, let us always keep in mind this simple A.A. paradox: by daily practice of our Twelve Step program, we are never in real danger of drinking. But with that dishonest little monkey ODAP around, we are never entirely safe."[4]

Let us examine this aspect of Webster's spirituality by tracing the emergence of the recovering personality throughout the Twelve Steps. It can be seen through quotations from the second (1947) printing of the *Interpretation*, its marginal annotations, and related ideas from *Our Devilish Alcoholic Personalities* (hereafter "*ODAP*"). In that book Webster actually personified those alcoholic traits with the name ODAP, sometimes letting that "devil" speak in a sardonic voice.

The personality change serves as the framework for insights into Webster's spirituality. Throughout his *Interpretation*, in both the text itself and Webster's marginal

95

annotations, we see references to the "alcoholic personality," and the recovering person's "new personality" in conjunction with a "new way of life." The many references to a "new personality" are in sharp contrast with the "old way of life" as outlined by the "devilish" alcoholic personality.

Prefacing the introduction to the 1947 printing of the *Interpretation*, Webster added a long marginal note:

> Last 13 years since advent [of] A.A. much progress/recovery made. Society has fair attitude alcoholic. A.A. provided means mass recovery. 50% alcoholics coming to A.A. never drink again—program works. If you are alcoholic—admit it—want quit—desire it above anything else. Not moral issues—a 3 phase disease. Here as Patients. Patient doesn't favor hospital—just reverse. A.A. same—No one big enough help A.A. —We are helped by our presence here. Can't add or detract from A.A. Since we are the patients—we must practice this program to get the A.A. vitamins necessary permanent sobriety. Nicollet chapter not interested in evangelism—not policing members. Meetings here—you attend them—not worried. If you stay away you lose.[5]

It is the above hastily written page that leads one to

believe Webster used this little volume, the second printing, with its marginal annotations, as his text and commentary for delivering his lectures to AA newcomers.

Step One

We admitted we were powerless over alcohol—
that our lives had become unmanageable.

Webster confines the study of Step One to the physical illness caused by alcoholism. The remedy takes the form of a Twelve Step Program. "This program amounts to a Way of Life" through which new wholesome personalities emerge: ". . . we live the A.A. program to develop normal, well-integrated personalities that exclude the use of the narcotic alcohol. Drugs prevent this change in personality. They warp our thinking. They too quickly become a substitute for alcohol and are decidedly habit forming for most of us."[6] In order to embrace the program as a Way of Life, "beginners must understand what alcoholism is. That understanding derives from a study of Chapter I. A.A. program—Can't control drinking, but can control our thinking," Webster noted in the margin, adding, "the 6 discussion classes not half as distracting as 10 minutes waiting for bar to open."[7]

> "Step One infuriated him," he wrote in
> *ODAP*. "He jumped up and down upon my
> back pounding me upon my head yelling his

objection into my ears. 'You are not sick! You are not powerless! Your life is not unmanageable! Suppose you did drink too much. All you need is some food and good night of rest, then you'll be okay.'"[8]

Step Two

Came to believe that a Power greater than ourselves could restore us to sanity.

In this chapter of the *Interpretation*, Webster addresses the mental illness of alcoholism. He contends that the word "insanity" best describes the state of the alcoholic's mental health. This mental illness is self-imposed, grounded in self-centeredness. Will power is not a factor in recovery except when it is surrendered to a Higher Power. "Harmony with God is the only hope of the alcoholic; it is possible by making A.A. your way of life. The acceptance and practice of the Twelve Steps of the A.A. program will give you a conscious contact with this Power Greater than yourself; it will restore you to sane thinking."[9] The word "harmony" caught on in the recovery field—harmony with God, with others, and with self.

"Sublimate our negative thinking thru willingness to submit to Power GTS," Webster noted later in the book's margin, abbreviating "greater than self."[10]

Step Two "enraged ODAP," Webster later wrote. "He used all of his under handed, cunning technique to discourage my acceptance of this Step. 'You're not insane. There's nothing wrong with your mind and don't let those A.A. nitwits tell you otherwise. It's a silly, insulting program, to say the least.'" [11]

Step Three
Made a decision to turn our will and our lives over to the care of God as we understood Him.

"Self-surrender of fear, pride, resentment, egotism, willfulness and all the undesirable traits that make up the personality of the alcoholic must be submitted to the care of God for supervision and reconstructive reconditioning," Webster wrote in the *Interpretation*. "... It is interesting to note that these members [who work the program] have exchanged their old alcoholic personalities for the sober, happy personality of the sincere A.A. member." He went on, "We regard the outcome of this Step in complete confidence, as we know from the example of other members that God's will can be understood, that our understanding of His care will give us new personalities that exclude alcohol—

Photo on next page: Webster's hand annotations on Step Three in his 1947 copy of the Interpretation.

over alcohol outweighed the regard we held for our own security or the good intentions toward our loved ones.

The remorse that drinking brought filled us with kindly intent toward deserving friends and relatives, but never allowed us to make permanent restitution. Resolutions and good intentions bolstered great faith within us during periods of sobriety, but being spiritually ill, we were unable to carry out our plans. Our "dog house" existence was occasionally relieved by sane and thoughtful acts during sober moments only to be resumed upon the next drunk, until we lost faith in ourselves. We were strong willed in all matters except in our ability to control our drinking, our drinking behavior, or our treatment of others.

It is not until we are fully aware of these facts that we become "fed up" with our inability to assume or execute normal responsibilities. It is only when we realize and admit the fact that "Our troubles were self imposed and that we were extreme examples of self will run riot" that we are ready to look outside ourselves for help.

Alcoholics who have accepted and practiced Step Three know the value of turning their will and their lives over to the care of God as they understand Him. Faith in the power of God, as they under-

[handwritten marginalia:] Alcoholic fellow with Both feet firmly planted in Mid air.

[handwritten marginalia:] Self Knowledge useless Without Outside Help.

[handwritten marginalia:] Then Pull ourself up Byour Boot Strap

[handwritten marginalia:] Living Evidence That Faith In Higher Power Works.

STEP THREE

[handwritten: Future revision]

stand Him, has brought them happiness and sobriety as it promoted recovery from the spiritual illness of alcoholism.

Some of us hesitated to face the requirements of
this step for <u>fear of public opinion</u> or because
it seemed hypocritical to turn to God for help after
ignoring Him for years.

[handwritten margin notes: Turning over To God / As we understand Him—Hard Because We / Be Self Centered / Too]

It is well to realize that we belong to an anonymous society; that the public has no way of knowing
what we are doing *except that we no longer drink.*
The fact is that although they did not accept us
while we drank, they will honor and receive us
when we stop.

[handwritten margin notes: —We Cant Seem To Accept The Effective Simplicity of Surrender]

We failed to stop of our own volition; we tried
devious way of controlling our drinking and to
regulate our lives; we did everything within our
power and knowledge to escape the effects of alcoholism.

The sensible thing to do now, if we are serious
about gaining permanent sobriety, is to surrender
our false pride, as thousands of other alcoholics
have done, and effect our recovery from alcoholism
under the care of GOD <u>as we understand Him.</u> The
fact that thousands of alcoholics have recovered
and that new hundreds are daily doing it by help
from a POWER GREATER THAN OURSELVES

[handwritten margin notes: Are We Ready To Proceed With childlike FAITH here Successful with This Program OR Will Prejudice / To Spiritual Contact / Continue / you In unmanageable, Self Centered—Drunkenness?]

personalities that do happily relate us to God, to a conventional world, and to our fellow men." [12]

In his margin notes, Webster observed that making this decision to turn our will and our lives over "follows much Study—Thought—Meditation." It is "thru Recognition of our need for help from 'Higher Power'—we develop sincerity, then take on Responsibility." [13]

His other notes include these:

- "Rationalization—Alibis of Alcoholic are handicaps to Spiritual Progress—They are products of self-will—Traits of the Alcoholic Personality—Obstructions to whole hearted application of a Higher Power. —Important we recognize devastating influence of world cares—Worry, Fear, Hatred make Step Three impossible." [14]

- "Humility—The Shortcut to understanding God." [15]

- "Habit is an important factor—Get the 24 hour habit—Practice happy relations with the 'Higher Power' —progressively thru meditation and Faithful, humble effort you will acquire a peace of Mind, satisfying beyond belief and in direct proportion to your Willingness to Possess it." [16]

Step Three bugged ODAP severely, said Webster. "You've done lots of idiotic things, but nothing like turning your life over to the care of God. . . You don't need God. What you need is a good psychiatrist. He'll give you the cause of alcoholism, *providing, of course you are really an alcoholic.* . . Read less and less in that A.A. Book, and more and more books on medicine and psychology. They have all your answers, ODAP told him."[17]

Step Four

Made a searching and fearless moral inventory of ourselves.

"The purpose of taking a moral inventory," Webster wrote, "is to expose the noxious traits of our alcoholic personalities, to eliminate them from the new personalities that with the help of the Alcoholics Anonymous Program as a 'Way of Life,' we now propose to develop. . . The AA usage of the term 'personality' deals with the development of new character traits necessary to our recovery from alcoholism. It has no relation to personal magnetism emanating from physical health, beauty, or charm."[18]

In a marginal annotation, Webster provides an overview: "Step Four starts education of your desires in right way. Desire sobriety—right motives—deal honorably with yourself. Learn how to live—then look forward to the adventure of living next 24 hours applying AA philosophy to your problems—the daily issues that confront you—not dodging them as we have in the past—learn proper use of dissatisfaction—intelligent desire for unselfish improvement."[19]

"The A.A. personality is characterized by composure, serenity, humility," he added on the next page, later observing the Fourth Step need for honesty—"Honesty with yourself, God, and with your fellowman."[20]

ODAP strongly disapproved Webster's carrying out the provisions of Step Four. "Better think hard before you act on this Step, old buddy, you can't record all of your bad actions. That's a negative approach. . . it's the wrong thing to do. . . you don't have to make a written inventory. A mental inventory is just as good. . .You have no flaws in your make-up. You are not a weakling like the other drunks in A.A. Be positive. Don't admit defeat. . . Leave out the bad points. Just list the good ones. You've got lots of them."[21]

Step Five

Admitted to God, to ourselves, and to another human being the exact nature of our wrongs.

"The metamorphosis from the alcoholic to the NEW A.A. PERSONALITY shows its first sign of life upon completion of Step Five," said Webster in the *Interpretation*.[22] He noted the Step's promise and pitfalls in his marginalia:

- "Admitting has definite Psychological [effects]

in recovery. Puts us in an attitude of Honesty and Humility—The basic requirements of the new AA Personality we wish to develop."[23]

- "Alcoholic personality traits die hard out of habit . . . can't rebuild overnight."[24] "Honesty, like humility, is crucial to recovery. It is Step V that initiates the spiritual awakening and is responsible for the willing attitude necessary for Steps 6 and 7."[25]

Vis-à-vis Step Five, ODAP directed his best verbal punches against Webster. "You can't trust your drinking history with another human being. Your record is too bad. You'll be lucky if they don't put you in jail. . . Why risk it? Why humiliate yourself. . . You are the only one who knows anything about your past behavior. Let the memories die a natural death. Why tell some disinterested clergyman about them?"[26]

Steps Six and Seven

Were entirely ready to have God remove all
these defects of character. Humbly asked
Him to remove our shortcomings.

Webster observed that, upon completion of the Fifth Step, "for the first time we are facing our REAL SELVES—the selves whose withered roots have touched and are now drawing upon an unfailing source of assurance, power and security."[27] Steps Six and Seven are the steps of "willingness and humility and contribute to the loss of self-centeredness," his annotations say. They are "decidedly helpful in full application of Step no. 3. They are surely a means of turning our will and lives over to care of God."[28]

Honesty and humility are two cornerstones for AA spirituality in general; and they were for Webster in particular. The cultivation of humility explicitly mentioned in the Seventh Step is the death warrant of self-centeredness. Webster noted that ODAP's "hypnotic power to dull our spiritual enthusiasm over Steps Six and Seven become a threat to our hopes for daily progress in A.A. . . He does this in a clever and convincing manner. . . He talks to us about the things we love to hear, and tells us that there is no need for further concern and instructs us the battle is won." Having "gotten rid of the alcoholic termites, don't become too concerned over a few helpless cockroaches. . . Slow up a bit. . . You're not supposed to become a saint. . . God knows you're human. 'He' forgives you and the A.A. members will take care of you if you get drunk. . . You can do a little social drinking when your business demands it. Drinking is no longer a problem for you. You've proved that you can take it or leave it alone."[29]

Steps Eight and Nine

Made a list of all persons we had harmed, and became
willing to make amends to them all. Made direct
amends to such people wherever possible, except when
to do so would injure them or others.

Both procrastination and the hasty application of these
Steps should be avoided. As Webster put it, "Some members
under inspiration of the new personalities they are creating
become emotional and act on the spur of the moment. Their
hasty action is apt to fall short of accomplishment."[30] These
two Steps regarding amends speak to self, others, and one's
Higher Power. Acceptance of the AA program as a way of
life requires that we make amends to others.

"We make amends to ourselves, to the personalities
we were before becoming alcoholic. . . Then there are the
amends we have to make to God. These become automatic;
they are the requirements of each of the Twelve Steps. The
AA program is ONE BIG AMEND broken up into twelve
parts."[31]

ODAP encourages the reluctance of newcomers to make
a list and subsequently to make amends. "You are not ready
to take this Step [8]. What's your hurry? . . . Suppose you
make such a list and your wife accidentally finds it. What
happens then? Your wife is pretty nosey, you know. . . . Don't
take a chance. Don't make a list. Whatever harm you have

done, it is over. . . . This Step may be for other alcoholics, but that list is not for you." Step Nine was made-to-order for ODAP's naysaying. "Don't complicate your effort to carry out this Step by calling upon a list of individuals. They are not interested in you, so stay away from them. . . .You are the only one to whom amends should be made, and you make them by showing your old friends you can drink with them like any normal person. Be a man, show the world that you can handle your liquor without getting into trouble. A.A. says you can't. You show them you can."[32]

Step Ten

Continued to take personal inventory and when
we were wrong promptly admitted it.

"Remember that any fool can defend his errors. Get out of that class. REMEMBER THAT YOUR NEW PERSONALITY IS NOT COMPATIBLE WITH MORAL DEFECTS OR CONCEALED ERRORS." In this Step, Webster points to the threefold relationship that is the essence of all spirituality. "Check yourself thoroughly. Don't make a farce out of your life. You owe it to God, yourself and your family [others] to make real headway. You must THINK SOBER and LIVE SOBER."[33]

Webster's margin notes: "A.A. calls #10 Step Action—Highlights—Inventory—continued correction of mistakes—

Code of Love and Tolerance—Miracle of Sobriety is ours—We are thinking right—We are not afraid of alcohol. . . . Drinking no longer a problem if we keep spiritually fit— Our daily reprieve is contingent on that condition. Cured of alcoholism—No. Working on our Will Power? Yes, with one condition—If every day— 'We carry the vision of God's will into all our activities.'"[34] Meanwhile, Webster observed ODAP: "The sinful little monkey rode my shoulder day and night . . . He was viciously intolerant of Step Ten. 'Who is kidding who? You made an inventory in Step Four. You listed names in Step Eight, and considered making amends in Step Nine. Must you become an A.A. accountant to succeed in this program? . . . Aren't you becoming rather sanctimonious by admitting your mistakes to everybody?'"[35]

Step Eleven

Sought through prayer and meditation to improve our conscious contact with God as we understood Him, praying only for knowledge of His will for us and the power to carry that out.

"Knowledge of the need for this Step is based on the past experience of A.A. members," warned Webster in the *Interpretation*. ". . .They have mistaken recovery for cure, so after

---

Photo on next page: Webster's commentary on Step Eleven in his 1947 copy of the Interpretation.

[handwritten marginalia: If Isn't Thinking about; Its Apt; That Is; Resentment; Dishonesty; for instance; Keep Higher Power; Courtesy; Humility; Watch Out for Complacency; Personality change; Stops; When We Take Over GOD's Duties]

[handwritten across top: Status Drinking again but rather; spiritual Illn]

drink again, we never even think about it." They let down their guard and ease up on spiritual contacts and service.

A positive attitude toward permanent sobriety is commendable. It is the attitude we wish all members to take. *[handwritten: but on 24 hr basis not a lifetime.]*

The fact we have no desire or intention to ever drink again is a favorable frame of mind for the new member to hold. It is our ambition, a mental condition to be grateful for, BUT ONE THAT TOO OFTEN FOSTERS COMPLACENCY WHICH CAN LEAD US INTO TROUBLE UNLESS GOD IS GIVEN FULL CREDIT FOR THE SOBRIETY WE ENJOY. *[handwritten: Should keep up Spiritual Discipline 24 hrs Daily.]*

When complacency develops we are apt to forget the part that God has played in effecting our rehabilitation. We overlook the fact that our nervous systems are still those of alcoholics. We seem to forget that as alcoholics we are susceptible to moods and emotions that we formerly appeased with alcohol. Complacency obscures the knowledge that our recovery from alcoholism was granted by a POWER GREATER THAN OURSELVES, that without contact with God, reversion to our old low physical and spiritual levels is probable.

Cooperation with a POWER GREATER THAN OURSELVES has pulled us out of the alcoholic rut.

STEP ELEVEN *Forwarned—Forarmed*

Step Eleven is a maintenance step that was planned
to keep us out and to make us stay put.

It keeps us spiritually active and in tune with
God. It insures against the dulling of inspiration as
our alcoholic problems diminish. *Think Our Problem Licked*

Understanding of this situation and the knowledge that members do get "off the beam" spiritually at times is our first line of defense. We fortify
this defense by keeping uppermost in our minds *Relate*
that "In reality we are on a DAILY REPRIEVE, *Experience*
that our reprieves are CONTINGENT UPON OUR *of Member*
SPIRITUAL CONDITION." *Confidentially*

The bitter experiences of members who insist up- *Assured*
on learning the hard way—the backsliders who re- *He'd Never*
turned to drinking—attest to the truth of this state- *Drink Again*
ment. *(Maybe)*

Invariably their trouble FIRST STARTS WITH *Drunk the*
NEGLECT OF PRAYER and matures when they *Next Week*
completely abandon conscious contact with God
and service to others.

Our realization of God's help in the past im- *How To*
presses us with the fact that it can be utilized to *Improve*
even better use in the future. A sure way of in- *Conscious*
creasing this help and expanding our contact with *Contact*
God is possible through simple prayers of sincere *with God*
appreciation. Meditate on the help He has given,
acknowledge its source, and be genuine in your

Should keep Self Centeredness Out of Picture

a few months of sobriety have considered practice of the A.A. philosophy unnecessary. . . . They take their changed personalities TOO MUCH FOR GRANTED, assuming that once acquired they will always stay with them."[36] Step Eleven "continues our personality change," he observed in his margin notes. "Keep Higher Power constantly in our picture. Watch out for complacency. Personality change stops when we take over God's duties. . . Make relaxation part of Personality Change. It is an important factor."[37]

"My opposition to Step 11 was overcome by thoughts of my helplessness and desperation before A.A.," Webster wrote later in *ODAP*. "I discussed this with my sponsor, who advised me to continue praying many times each day. . . . There was no delayed action after I gave Step Eleven a fair trial. It was truly a stimulating experience. Over-night, my whole concept of life started to change for the better. It gave me a zest for living, honestly and unselfishly which I had never had before. . . . ODAP, who had been hiding in the shadow of my insane behavior for so many years knew my weakness and my inconsistency to carry out a good intention. . . He seized upon daily meditation as the weapon with which to deter my well-intentioned advance toward successful application of this Step. 'Why don't you put off this early morning prayer business until noon? . . . What about God's will? Did he ever get you any big business accounts, or did you get them yourself by drinking with your customers?

You'd better give this matter some thought. Your A.A. principles could easily lose business for you.'"38

Step Twelve

Having had a spiritual awakening as the result of these steps, we tried to carry this message to alcoholics, and to practice these principles in all our affairs.

"In arriving at a true picture of this A.A. metamorphosis it is helpful to reflect upon our spiritual experience as stepping stones to the NEW PERSONALITIES we gain by daily practice of the Twelve Steps," Webster wrote. ". . . We have developed God conscious personalities sufficient to effect our recovery from alcoholism . . . The outcome of our improved spiritual status and the service we render others is not without benefit. God finally declares a dividend, not in the coin of man, but in the Divine Currency of Serenity. We are allowed to draw upon an infinite store of harmony and well-being. We become at peace with the world."39

"God does not force us to live the Twelve Steps. He simply grants us sobriety if we are consistent in their daily practice. . . . Fear, dishonesty, resentment and reservation are a few of the mental blocks which impede our progress in the A.A. way of life. These emotions often cause us to drink again. ODAP knows this. . . Step Twelve presents a favorite field of malicious sabotage for him. 'What do you know about spiritual awakening? Aren't you just using an expression which you heard in A.A.? . . . The only spirits you are familiar with are those you got from alcohol and they put you to sleep, they didn't awaken you. Remember? . . . As for practicing the Twelve Step principles in all your affairs, it can't be done, so why wear yourself out trying to achieve such an improbable undertaking?'"[40]

Webster ends his essay with an important reflection: "For the purpose of identification and comparison, I have used the analogy of two opposite powers in the A.A. Fellowship to emphasize the help of a Higher Power, and the barriers which ODAP builds up to obstruct our efforts to live a normal, sober life. . . . Even so, let us always keep in mind this simple A.A. paradox: by daily practice of our Twelve Step program, we are never in real danger of drinking. But with that dishonest little monkey ODAP around, we are never entirely safe."[41]

The following chart may help the reader understand the disparate relationships between the Old and New Personalities:

Alcoholic Personality	Recovering Personality
Self-Centeredness	Humility
Resentments	Acceptance
Fear	Trust/Hope
Dishonesty	Honesty
Bedevilments	Promises
Self-Will	God's Will

In his book *Back to Basics*, Wally P. aligns the personality traits in the chart above in the following manner: "Let's look at the third sentence again. It reads, 'Where had we been selfish, dishonest, self-seeking and frightened?' These short-comings are based on self-will. In addition, they are the opposites of the Four Standards of Honesty, Purity, Unselfishness and Love, which is used as a test for God's Will."[42]

9

The Spirituality of Surrender

One way to understand the Steps within the context of recovery is to isolate Step Three—*Made a decision to turn our will and our lives over to the care of God* as we understood Him—and Step Eleven—*Sought through prayer and meditation to improve our conscious contact with God* as we understood Him, *praying only for knowledge of His will for us and the power to carry that out.* These two Steps can act as cords, weaving all the Steps together. They serve as the centerpiece of recovery. These two Steps were obviously important to Webster, as they are the ones most heavily annotated in the 1947 printing of the *Interpretation*.

On the anniversary of his recovery, Webster wrote to Dr. Bob, attesting to his growth in spirituality and revealing to him "what it was like, what happened and what it is like now." Faith and love had replaced fear:

> Five years ago today, Friday came the same as this year on the 13th which means little to you but to me it's a Great Day as it was then that I entered Alcoholics Anonymous.

There was no energy left in my spirit, mind or body. I was truly a sick, defeated man, floundering helplessly in the mire of alcoholism. Physical illness, fear and despair soon gave way to hope, harmony and accomplishment as the Twelve Steps revealed themselves to me. Thru understanding and application of these Steps I learned to link my energies to the calm of God's purposes and found the peace of His power. He has replaced the false energy of fear with the true energy of faith working thru love. Love of God and love of my fellow man. Thank you, Dr. Bob, for blazing the trail that made this possible.

I have tried to pay back in a small measure, some of the benefits A.A. has given me. The hours spent in doing this have only obligated me more as each new effort on my part has brought new reward.

This appreciation of God's presence and help was at the bottom of the Twelve Step *Interpretation.* The purpose was long range sponsorship. It started in a small way with the boys in our group but has extended beyond that as a few other clubs seem to be using the little book as an outline for study of the

AA book. The demand is not great but the
satisfaction is as I feel that others are getting
a little help because of my co-operation with
God, who saw fit to permit it."[1]

For Webster it was simple and clear that the integrity
of the new personality would be maintained by living the
Twelve Steps daily, especially in the decision to turn our will
over to God (Step Three) and praying only for knowledge of
his will for us (Step Eleven). Spirituality evolves through the
interplay of those two energies—God's will and our will—
by turning our will over to the care of God. For many this
saying is hard—who can live by it? Still, an understanding
of these two Steps and their interplay in our lives highlight
the spirituality of the program, recovery, and the transpar-
ency of the new personality.

How do we know that we are practicing Step Three,
truly turning our will over? The simple answer appears to
be when we are living Steps Four through Twelve, repairing
and nurturing the relationship with ourselves, with others,
and with the God of our understanding. That is the AA
way of life.

The AA program worked for Webster because he was
able to grasp and internalize the over-arching principle
of the program found throughout *The Little Red Book,* but
especially in Steps Three and Eleven—that of surrender—
surrender of the alcoholic personality at the root of which

was self-centeredness. This was the fundamental principle that Webster believed would maintain the integrity of the new personality, which lived by other-centeredness—humility. It was the mortar that anchored all the Steps. Webster wrote in the *Interpretation*, "A.A., as a 'Way of Life,' is basically a spiritual program that arrests alcoholism as we develop within ourselves a true sense of responsibility to God and to those we have harmed by our uncontrolled drinking."[2]

We have briefly covered all of the Steps in illustrating the contrast between the Alcoholic Personality and the new Recovering Personality that emerges with the practice of the Twelve Steps. Concentrating here on Steps Three and Eleven allows us to gain a fundamental grasp of both the idea and reality of surrender. How did Webster interpret "making a decision to turn over our will" (Step Three), and "praying only for knowledge of His Will for us" (Step Eleven)? The relationship between our will and God's will is *the* spiritual question that has bedeviled theologians and lay people for centuries. Outrageous claims and atrocities as well as extraordinary acts of compassion and sacrifice for others on behalf of God's will continue to this day. How did AA present a solution for the alcoholic? Webster shared some of his answers in a letter to Dr. Bob:

> This habit of living consciously, daily with God gives us strength for enduring that which has to be endured, energy for going ahead

when the going is tough, insight into that which is *doable* (?)[illegible] and wisdom for planning the right way. Personally I have the Twelve Steps of A.A. to thank for recognition of the above fact and the degree of peace of mind and contented sobriety it has brought me. Your part in this Bob is not over looked. God and His agents share my appreciation.[3]

"Made a decision to turn our will . . . over to the care of God . . ."

What makes it so difficult to breach the walls of the alcoholic personality? It is protected by the moat of self-absorption and all those derivative defects cultivated during its drinking career, especially dishonesty. Webster was absolutely clear about this in his Third Step presentation. The alcoholic was "the great/perfect example of self-will run riot," he said. "Making a decision to turn our wills and lives over"—surrender— is the perfect antidote to the affliction of self-centeredness. It is relatively easy to find those places where surrender is explicitly mentioned, and turning our will over is to surrender. But the ultimate questions are: what does it mean to turn our will over? What is the relationship between our will and God's will? How does free will fit into the picture? How do I know what God's will is for me? The following are a few brief references to surrender found in Webster's marginal notes on the Third Step in the *Interpretation*:

> It is hard to turn our will over to God as we understand Him because we are too self-centered and cannot accept the effective simplicity of *surrender*. It is a decision that can only follow upon much study, thought, and meditation. The sensible thing to do, as thousands of alcoholics have discovered, is to swallow our false pride and entrust ourselves to the guidance of God as we understand him by practicing Steps Four through Twelve. Rationalizations and alibis, the products of self-will and the traits of the alcoholic personality are the handicaps to spiritual progress. A.A. members who are doing their best to learn the meaning of God's will have exchanged their old alcoholic personality for the sober happy personality of the sincere A.A. members.
>
> The new member of AA is like a soldier who is given his equipment. He doesn't question anything—he simply learns how to use it. Reliance on self-will becomes less difficult when we consider the role that it has played in messing up our lives. Any will other than our own could have regulated our lives to better

advantage. We come to a better understanding of the Third Step when we practice the Twelfth Step. In helping others find solutions to their problems we can easily come to a better grasp of our own and the answers to them are more easily accessible.

Finally, humility is the short cut to understanding God's will for us.

The following reflections on humility and the "will to drink" are offered as suggestions for a fuller understanding of the practical application of Step Three.

Humility and Other-Centeredness

Humility is the cornerstone, the spinal cord of other-centeredness. How are we to understand this? The variety of descriptions and definitions of humility makes it difficult to get a handle on this quality that creates the background of the Seventh Step: "Humbly ask Him to remove our shortcomings," a request whose original version suggested that it be done on our knees. Throughout *The Little Red Book*, Webster proposes that humility combined with honesty is the spiritual remedy for self-centeredness.

It is this author's belief that humility, when understood correctly, speaks to the "other centeredness," which ultimately is the God of our understanding. As I wrote in *The Essence of Twelve Step Recovery*, humility takes on a variety of meanings and is oftentimes difficult to define or describe. "Even the dictionary shows the same trepidation in defining humility, describing this quality by what it is not (for example it is not characterized by arrogance or grandiosity, substitute self-centeredness). Etymologically it derives from the Latin word *humus*, which means ground or earth. According to the Torah, when God made man he molded him from the earth (this is addressed in the prayer from Ash Wednesday: 'Remember that from dirt you have come and to dirt you shall return') and then breathed His Spirit into him, thus giving him life. In this sense, humility means the acceptance of one's *dependence* upon a God of one's understanding and the acceptance of a role of equality (neither superiority nor inferiority) with the rest of creation (the rest of the earth—humus). In Jewish writings, the honest man is described as one practicing justice and compassion and who 'walks humbly with one's God.'"

As such, "humility serves as the foundation for all the Steps in the acceptance of the 'we' principle: 'I cannot do it by myself; I need the God of my understanding and others to help me.'"[4]

Embracing this description of humility allows us to understand how it lies at the bottom of surrender and enhances its employment in the Seventh Step. The cultivation of humility in our daily lives allows us to move easily from compliance to surrender. We no longer go through the motions in the practice of the Steps, for humility aligns our heads with our hearts.

"The Will to Drink": Webster's Commentary on the Third Step from *Stools and Bottles*

"Turning one's will over" may seem a relatively benign concept, but it can be demoralizing for some. The freedom of one's will is a precious gift. What are the practical implications for the alcoholic? What softens the Step for many is the realization that we are turning our wills over to the "*care* of God" not to the "*control*" of God, which guarantees the continued freedom of our personal wills. In 1952, Webster described the evolution of his own thinking in a letter to Bill W.:

> My observation of many members who really try to fit Step Three into their lives has been that they seem to have a funny conception of what is expected. They concentrate so hard on trying to find tangible evidence of God that they never really make an honest decision or come to the realization He is to be found in daily living of the 12 Steps. This bothered me for months. The result was the revision of Step Three. I relieved my mind by trying to simplify the former matter but now

in reviewing my efforts feel that the job was
far from adequate.[5]

With the publication of *Stools and Bottles* in 1955,
Webster provided a "more adequate," simple, even singular
understanding for those having trouble with the Third Step.

There are two things to remember about *Stools and
Bottles*. First, it was published two years after Bill W.'s *Twelve
Steps and Twelve Traditions*. Second, the essay on the Third
Step, with its very practical approach, stands in sharp contrast to Bill W.'s chapter on the Third Step, with its emphasis
on "willingness" as the key that opens the door to that Step.
In *Stools and Bottles*, Webster expanded upon the meaning
and practice of the Third Step to accompany what he had
already written in *The Little Red Book*. His suggestions for a
further understanding of the "working mechanics" of Step
Three were both practical and relevant for those struggling
to implement Step Three in their lives. Webster provided the
key to open the door that let the spirit and the sunshine in.

He wrote that Step Three provides a simple solution for
the spiritual illness that resides in alcoholism. While the
solution is simple, it remains difficult for some. "Its success
lies in our willingness to discipline our minds with spiritual
thinking. Indifference and prejudice are the chief barriers to
success. Alcoholic minds rebel against the surrender which
this Step suggests."[6]

Those who have failed in AA forget their road maps and wind up in the wrong place. This happens when compliance replaces surrender. In *Stools and Bottles*, Webster writes, "There is a great difference between agreeing with Step Three and in trying to live it. A dangerous difference for an alcoholic, for one is compliance—the other surrender. Alcoholics comply, but fight surrender."[7]

Throughout his presentation on this section of the Third Step—the "decision to turn over our will"—Webster emphasizes the phrase "will to drink." Here are some selections:

- "The truth is—'We *will* to drink when and where we choose, resigned to drinking's penalties.'"[8]

- "The will of the drinking alcoholic seems to point in one direction—toward the bottle."[9]

- "On occasion our will to drink amounted to an obsession and always ended in trouble."[10]

- "It is only when we make our lives a channel for His Will that He grants us contented sobriety. His will regenerates us. Our will to drink can only destroy us."[11]

- "Thus enlightened about our will and the inward thoughts which mold our destiny, we are ready to turn our will, to drink at any cost, over to the care of 'God as we understand Him.'"[12]

- "Step Three adds the third leg to our recovery stool. Its simple requirement is a final decision to surrender our will to drink to 'God as we understand Him' and to gain our understanding of him by living the 12 Steps."[13]

Once we surrender our lives and our will to drink over to God as we understand Him, the implementation of Steps Four through Twelve guarantees that we will not compromise that surrender.

"Praying only for knowledge of His will for us. . ."

The printed text of the *Interpretation* (second edition), and Webster's margin notes in his own copy, reveal his growing understanding of the important issue of knowledge of God's will.

"The question that has repeatedly confronted members is—WHAT IS GOD'S WILL?—HOW AM I TO KNOW IT FROM MY OWN WILL?" the *Interpretation* asks. "We do not attempt to answer this question directly. It is not our responsibility. It is the duty of the church and organized religion to interpret God's will. . . ."[14] But Webster's handwritten note adds, "One thing is sure. Alcoholism is not God's will.

Certainly self-centeredness is not God's will. Practicing the Twelve Steps will develop knowledge of God's will for us."[15]

It is in this last sentence that Webster provides the best and simplest answer to that perennial question that has haunted men and women throughout the centuries—*How do I know that it is God's will for me? How do I surrender to it?* For alcoholics it was simple—they know that alcoholism is not God's will, and that they *are* following God's will when they practice Steps Four through Twelve. Sponsors and the group become the sounding boards for any further questions.

Webster then provides more food for thought in discerning God's will. "We, therefore, deduct that our understanding of God's will IS TO BE FOUND IN OUR ATTITUDE TOWARDS OUR FELLOW MEN AND IN THE TREATMENT WE ACCORD THEM," reads the text.[16] And, Webster added: "This treatment has to do largely with proper discipline of our emotional lives. Are we to remain extreme examples of self will run riot? Or will we gain a knowledge of God's will by fully accepting Step Three and the practice of turning our will over to Him?"[17]

On the next page, the *Interpretation* reads, "WE ARE, TO THE BEST OF OUR ABILITY AND KNOWLEDGE, GAINING AN UNDERSTANDING OF GOD'S WILL THROUGH THE SERVICE WE RENDER OTHERS."[18] In the margin, Webster had already written: "Remember we are alcoholics—banded together to acquire contented sobriety. Part of our treatment is helping the other fellow."[19]

Understanding God's will for us comes with little effort when we are helping our family and friends and helping new members seek recovery in the Fellowship. This is the Love and Service couplet stressed by Dr. Bob.

Step Eleven continues to deal with self-centeredness on a daily basis. Prayer and meditation and the cultivation of humility strengthen our decision to turn our will and lives over to the care of God. Webster believed that Step Eleven continued the personality change and that its omission was a direct shortcut to drunkenness. It was easy to take things for granted, to let one's guard down, to rest on one's oars. One had to watch out for complacency. Webster jotted in one margin note, "Personality change stops when we take over God's duties."[20]

Webster made a strong pitch for praying and meditating when one is relaxed and composed and not tense and fatigued. He urges readers to regard relaxation as a very important part of their personality change. He made a "daily physical audit" part of the thirty-one daily meditations offered in *Stools and Bottles*.

"In reality we are on a DAILY REPRIEVE, that our reprieves are CONTINGENT UPON OUR SPIRITUAL CONDITION," said Webster in the *Interpretation*. "The bitter experience of members who insist upon learning the hard way—the backsliders who returned to drinking—attest to the truth of this statement."[21]

How, then, should we pray?

Webster has provided us with two examinations of the prayer life, apparently based on his own practice and daily regimen. The first is the reflections on the Lord's Prayer found in *Our Devilish Alcoholic Personalities*, which was published in 1970, the year before he died. A second source of Webster's ascetical practices is the prayers and meditations found in the last section of *Stools and Bottles*. In addition to Webster's essays on the first three Steps, *Stools and Bottles* also provides a companion piece for the implementation of the Eleventh Step—the month-long schedule of prayers and meditations at the end of this volume. As mentioned earlier, the format that Webster uses somewhat resembles the one employed by Richmond Walker in his book *Twenty-Four Hours a Day,* and both made the theme of the two selves (personalities) an essential topic of their writings. Webster and Walker felt the transformative process of Alcoholics Anonymous in the same way—through practicing the Twelve Steps in all their affairs.

Webster himself held *Twenty-Four Hours a Day* in some esteem, believing its contents to be of great value to the recovering community. That may or may not have been the reason that Webster incorporated thirty-one meditations into his *Stools and Bottles.* In any case, they provide some further insights into how he viewed prayer and meditation. Each day consists of a daily reminder, a daily inventory, a suggested meditation, a spiritual contact (prayer), and a daily physical audit. (Webster recognized the importance of periods of daily relaxation.) The following are a few selections.

In the suggested meditation for the third day in *Stools and Bottles*, Webster appears to emphasize the idea of *willingness*—the concept Bill W. referred to as the formula for living the Third Step. Webster wrote, "Could God in His dealing with A.A. have said, 'Show me your willingness to live in sobriety and I will perform the miracle of contented sobriety in your lives.'"[22]

"How about self-centeredness, will it ruin us?" asks the daily inventory for the fifth day. "Do we live unstable lives? Is today the time to stop this 'I' complex and start living in terms of 'We'?"[23]

The suggested meditation for the seventeenth day is on the subject of "slips," a matter of serious concern to Webster and all the Nicollet Club members. "All slips are serious—some fatal. Those called minor are unfinished drunks. They will be completed later. Dishonesty in some form is the basis of a slip. This member should have confessed to his group. As A.A. patients, our minds are still alcoholic. We think in terms of drinking if we cannot be honest with ourselves. Slippers are ill. A.A. cannot forgive an illness, but it can help sick members to get well."[24]

The meditation for the twenty-third day of the month lays to rest any confusion over the meaning of the word "principles" in the Twelfth Step and the need to practice them in all our affairs.[25] It has become quite fashionable today to interpret the Twelfth Step phrase "practice these principles in all our affairs" as something other than the Twelve Steps themselves. It is misleading to write or talk about the principles of honesty, humility, courage, and trust as though these and not the Steps are the "guides to progress." Indeed Step Three as a principle of action requires the practice of all the qualities of humility, honesty, trust, and so forth.

The meditation for the twenty-fourth day of the month declares that "Our only authority is God's Will activating the conscience of our groups—His voice speaking through A.A. to the alcoholics who still suffer."[26]

"The truly great members of A.A. are all humble members," says the meditation for the twenty-seventh day of the month. "They give freely of their talent, but seek no praise. The publicity seeker is different. He lacks humility and openly courts acclaim but never seems to feel small about it. We can be either great or small in A.A., but as we sacrifice our vanities upon the altar of A.A. service we will rise and grow in stature and gain recognition without seeking it."[27]

The contents for each day are simple, unpretentious, and provide refreshing insights into the program and our relationship with the God of our understanding.

On Humility

Webster saw humility as the foundation of relational spirituality. In this third volume of *Bulletin Thirteen* (bulletins written to enlarge upon the spirituality of the Big Book and *The Little Red Book*), he wrote that humility allows us to undertake a true evaluation of conditions as they really are and to understand the proper relationship between ourselves and a Higher Power and between ourselves and our fellow man.

But first it takes true humility to admit one's alcoholism and remove the boulders of pride and arrogance that protect the alcoholic personality.

True humility also nourishes our understanding of our dependence upon help from a Higher Power, which is the essence of humility.

Humility in action is understanding our relationship with our fellow man and the acceptance and practice of good works in this relationship throughout every twenty-four-hour period. This is also the test of our humility.

—

God's Will—Man's Will

This relationship between man's will and God's will has been the subject of theological, philosophical, and spiritual discussion throughout the centuries. It has caused individuals much anguish. It has led to wars between nations and cultures. Prophets, religious founders, and reformers have sustained their teachings by relating them to God's will. Some of the most heinous activities promoted by the leaders of so-called religious reform movements have been carried out because "God wills it." The haunting question is: "How does one discern God's will?"

I recall my own life as a Franciscan for some thirty years. Before making my final commitment to the Franciscan way of life, I spent many years training, studying, and reflecting on the demands required of those wishing to live a Franciscan life. I finally made the commitment to embrace this way of life by consenting to live vows of poverty, chastity, and obedience. This meant turning my life and will over to the care of God as I then understood Him. Obedience, the last mentioned of the vows, was the easiest, and, at the same time, the most difficult. It was the easiest because I was to discover the will of God in the rule that St. Francis composed in order to follow the way of life proposed by the Gospel. Then if there were any question as to what the rule meant and how it was to be applied in a contemporary situation, my Superior was there to interpret it for me. This became sticky at times, especially when my interpretation was clearly at odds with his. But there could be no question that he was laying out God's will for me under the vow of obedience that I had taken. Surrender was made easy, but in reality, surrender is never easy and requires a daily offering of one's self.

"Praying only for knowledge of His will for us" is what is known in spiritual circles as the principle and practice of discernment—that is, searching out God's will for us. In order to discern God's will, alcoholics have four sources of energy into which they can tap. The first is prayer and meditation, listening, like the prophet, in the silent caves of our hearts for God's whisperings. The second source is the action of confiding in another (a trusted and wise sponsor) who has won our respect as a person conversant with the things of the Spirit as presented in the Twelve Steps. The third is sharing our thoughts with a small group of recovering people who have our trust in spiritual matters and whose questions about our spiritual dilemma will help point us in the right direction during our spiritual journey. No one is sitting in judgment. The best input is when members of the group share their own experiences instead of proposing solutions. The large AA meeting is not always the best venue for this. But sojourners are free to select some of the group with whom they wish to share their spiritual dilemma. Finally, the final source is to seek direction from within, tapping into our own personal resources, conscious of our strengths, and aware of our weaknesses. What is our real self saying to us? All four sources are at the beck and call of members of the Fellowship as they continue on their recovery journey. Spirituality is entered into through our relationships with self, with others, and with the God of our understanding. And that is what *The Little Red Book* is all about.

—

Notes

Abbreviations

HPA: Hazelden-Pittman Archives, housed at Hazelden Foundation, Center City, Minnesota.

Interpretation: Abbreviated title for *An Interpretation of the Twelve Steps of the Alcoholics Anonymous Program.* This was *The Little Red Book*'s title in its first printings, from 1946 to 1948. Even at that time, however, it was informally known as "the little red book." That name was adopted as its official title starting in 1949.

Introduction

1. See Wally P., *Back to Basics: The Alcoholics Anonymous Beginners' Meetings* (Tucson, AZ: Faith with Works Publishing, 2006), chapter 1.
2. Glenn Chesnut provides the best overview of the book's earliest years in his essay "The First Edition of the Little Red Book," Hindsfoot Foundation, http://hindsfoot.org /ed02.html.

Chapter 1

1. Copies of Chan Foreman's letters are in the Hazelden-Pittman Archives (hereafter HPA), box 77.

2. Foreman's address to Nicollet Club on occasion of Collins's 27th anniversary, HPA, Box 77.

3. Copy of Pat Cronin talk (date unknown), HPA, Box 77, courtesy of Jerry Oys.

4. Richmond Walker, *Twenty-Four Hours a Day,* Thoughts for the Day, entries for July 29, 30, and 31.

5. Pat Cronin talk (cited above).

6. Ibid.

7. Edward A. Webster, *Our Devilish Alcoholic Personalities* (Minnesota: Hamar Publishers, 1970) 23–4.

Chapter 2

1. Ruth Hock to Pat Cronin, Aug. 15, 1940, copy in possession of Jerry Oys, archivist.

2. HPA, Box 77 contains a large collection of documents, correspondence, and other papers connected with the history of the Nicollet Club and Barry Collins.

3. *Bulletin 13,* Vol. III, 1953. This small tract was Nicollet's newsletter through which Webster intended to implement Step Twelve, "carrying the message." HPA, Box 77.

4. HPA, Box 77.

5. *An Interpretation of the Twelve Steps of Alcoholics Anonymous*, second printing, 1947, 13.

6. *Grapevine* (Sept. 1945), as quoted in Wally P., *Back to Basics,* 2.

7. Unpublished draft of anniversary booklet, HPA, Box 77.

8. HPA, Box 77.

9. *Dr. Bob and the Good Oldtimers* (New York: Alcoholics Anonymous World Services, Inc., 1980), 300.

10. Forrest Richeson, *Courage to Change: Beginnings, Growth and Influence of Alcoholics Anonymous in Minnesota* (Minnesota: M & M Printing, 1978), 122.

11. Ibid., 122.

12. Ibid., 121.

13. *Dr. Bob and the Good Oldtimers*, 88.

14. Ibid., 85.

15. *Back to Basics*, 20.

16. First International A.A. Convention, Cleveland, Ohio, Sunday, July 30, 1950.

Chapter 3

1. Most of the details surrounding Webster's life are from conversations and notes from Webster's daughter, Lavina, and Webster's final published work, *Our Devilish Alcoholic Personalities*, 11–27.

2. Wally P., *Back to Basics*, 15–6. See also HPA, Box 77 for a copy of Burgher's letter.

3. Talk by Dr. T.A. Pincock, Twenty-fifth Annual Manitoba Conference in Winnipeg, 1969, HPA, Box 77.

4. *Our Devilish Alcoholic Personalities*, 26. On another set of page proofs Dr. Bob had written "Best wishes for continued success."

5. Dr. Bob to Ed Webster, Nov. 3, 1946 and December 29, 1946, HPA, Box 49.

6. Trysh Travis, *Language of the Heart: A Cultural History of the Recovery Movement from Alcoholics Anonymous to Oprah Winfrey* (University of North Carolina Press: Chapel Hill, 2009), 139.

Chapter 4

1. Glenn Chesnut, *The Little Red Book*, First Editions, Alcoholics Anonymous History, Hindsfoot Foundation.

2. Copies of the correspondence between the two can be found in the HPA, Box 49. Another cache of Webster's papers, which this writer was not able to access, resides with Jack H. in Arizona.

3. Webster to Dr. Bob, Dec. 13, 1946, HPA, Box 49.

4. Dr. Bob to Ed Webster, Dec. 29, 1946, HPA, Box 49.

5. Webster to Dr. Bob, Mar. 2, 1947, HPA, Box 49.

6. Webster to Dr. Bob, Mar. 19, 1947, HPA, Box 49.

7. *Dr. Bob and the Good Oldtimers*, 300.

8. Webster to Dr. Bob, May 15, 1949, HPA, Box 49.

9. Webster to Dr. Bob, Nov. 15, 1949, HPA, Box 49.

10. Bill W. to Webster, Nov. 14, 1946, HPA, Box 49.

11. Webster to Bill W., Dec. 10, 1947, HPA, Box 49.

12. Webster to Bill W., Sept. 6, 1948, HPA, Box 49.

13. Bill W. to Ed Webster, May 31, 1949, HPA, Box 49.

14. Editorial on the First Tradition: *Grapevine* 4, no. 7 (Dec. 1947): 2.

15. Webster to Bill W., Dec. 10, 1949, HPA, Box 49.

Chapter 5

1. Bill W. to Ed Webster, Nov. 14, 1946, HPA, Box 49.

2. Bill W. to Ed Webster, May 31, 1949, HPA, Box 49.

3. Bill W. to Barry Collins, Nov. 1950, quoted in *Aquebogue* (a pamphlet on Step Twelve, author unknown but likely Bill Pittman), 12–13, HPA, Box 49.

4. Bill W. to Clem L., Feb. 28, 1950, AA Archives, Box 26.

5. Bill W. to Clark R., Aug. 13, 1950, AA Archives, Box 26, 10.21.

6. Bill W. to Ed W. (not Ed Webster), Nov. 15, 1950, Box 26, 10.21.

7. Ed Webster to Bill W., Nov. 26, 1950, Minnesota-Minneapolis folder, Nicollet Group, G. 1.

8. Webster to Bill W., Nov. 28, 1950, AA Archives, Box 71, Folder G. 1, 131. The issue of the AA Directory became a thorn in Webster's side. On August 3, 1952 he wrote to the secretary of the New York Office: "Will you ask Bill. . . if they wish me to mail those 600 copies (Bulletin 13?) out to A.A. groups other than those we are dealing with?" He received a sharp reply: "It always seems to fall to my lot to write you somewhat disagreeable letters. . . but there are certain policies, Ed, which must be adhered to if there is to be any consistency in what we do.—That would involve Group Directory which is not to be used as a mailing list for any purpose whatever, no matter how worthy the cause . . . There seems to be no question as to the value of the Little Red Book and its widespread use. Frankly, I don't think there are too many groups that don't know of it.

Information concerning it has spread by word of mouth
. . . " Ann MacFarlane to Webster, Aug. 19, 1952, AA
Archives, Box 71, Nicollet Group folder, G.1.

9. Ed Webster to Bill W., Dec. 8, 1950, Minnesota-
Minneapolis folder, Nicollet Group, G.1.

10. Bill W. to Roy H., Dec. 21, 1950, AA Archives, Box 26,
10.21.

11. See Trish Travis, *The Language of the Heart,* 137 and
following pages. This book allowed me to explore this
issue in some depth. See her references to the New York
AA Archives, particularly in chapter 3, "Reading the
Language of the Heart," page 137 and its corresponding
references. Between the AA Archives and the Hazelden-
Pittman Archives, which contain the Webster correspondence, I was able to chronologically trace the textbook
issue. It is up to the reader to judge Bill W.'s forthrightness,
or lack thereof, in his dealings with Webster and *The Little
Red Book.*

12. Ed Webster to Bill W., Feb. 15, 1952, HPA, Box 49.

13. Bill W. to Ed Webster, Aug. 8, 1952, HPA, Box 49.

14. *Dr. Bob and the Good Oldtimers,* 325.

15. Ed Webster to Bill W., August 10, 1953, HPA, Box 49.

Chapter 6

1. See Damian McElrath, *Making the Little Black Book:
Inside the Working Manuscript of Twenty-Four Hours a Day*
(Center City, MN: Hazelden, 2012).

2. While Webster's daughter believed that he did lecture at Hazelden, the few who worked there during those years do not remember ever hearing Webster speak.

3. Copies of Webster-Hazelden contract papers, HPA, Box 77.

4. Damian McElrath, "Hazelden's Educational Mission and the Hazelden Pittman Archives" (unpublished manuscript, 2001) contains a lengthy biographical essay on Bill Pittman.

5. Ibid.

6. The Hazelden-Pittman Archives contain the following printings of *The Little Red Book:* first (1946), second (1947), fourth (1949), ninth (1953), twelfth (1957), fourteenth (1960), fifteenth (1962), eighteenth (1963), and a photocopy of the twenty-first printing (1967).

Chapter 7

1. *An Interpretation of the Twelve Steps of Alcoholics Anonymous* (hereafter *Interpretation*), Webster's margin notes, 52.

2. *Alcoholics Anonymous,* 4th ed., 83.

3. Damian McElrath, *The Essence of Twelve Step Recovery: Take It to Heart* (Center City, MN: Hazelden, 2009), 19–20.

4. Ibid.

5. Carl Jung, *Modern Man in Search of a Soul* (New York: Harcourt, Brace and Company, 1933), 173.

Chapter 8

1. *Our Devilish Alcoholic Personalities*, 29.
2. Maria Nemeth, Ph.D., *The Energy of Money: A Spiritual Guide to Financial and Personal Fulfillment* (New York: Ballantine, l999), 27.
3. *Our Devilish Alcoholic Personalities*, 56.
4. Ibid., 58.
5. *Interpretation*, Webster's margin notes, 8.
6. *Interpretation*, 18, 25.
7. *Interpretation*, Webster's margin notes, 19.
8. *Our Devilish Alcoholic Personalities*, 32.
9. *Interpretation*, 28.
10. *Interpretation*, Webster's margin notes, 27.
11. *Our Devilish Alcoholic Personalities*, 32.
12. *Interpretation*, 38, 40, 45.
13. *Interpretation*, Webster's margin notes, 35.
14. Ibid., 38.
15. Ibid., 39.
16. Ibid., 45.
17. *Our Devilish Alcoholic Personalities*, 33–4.
18. *Interpretation*, 47.
19. *Interpretation*, Webster's margin ntoes, 46.
20. Ibid., 47, 52.
21. *Our Devilish Alcoholic Personalities*, 35–6.
22. *Interpretation*, 69.

23. *Interpretation*, Webster's margin notes, 66.

24. Ibid., 67.

25. Ibid., 69.

26. *Our Devilish Alcoholic Personalities*, 36–7.

27. *Interpretation*, 71.

28. *Interpretation*, Webster's margin notes, 71, 72.

29. *Our Devilish Alcoholic Personalities*, 37–9.

30. *Interpretation*, 79.

31. Ibid., 86.

32. *Our Devilish Alcoholic Personalities*, 39–41.

33. *Interpretation*, 95.

34. *Interpretation*, Webster's margin notes, 88–9.

35. *Our Devilish Alcoholic Personalities*, 42–3.

36. *Interpretation*, 97.

37. *Interpretation*, Webster's margin notes, 97, 98, 102.

38. *Our Devilish Alcoholic Personalities*, 44–47.

39. *Interpretation*, 114–116.

40. *Our Devilish Alcoholic Personalities*, 49–52.

41. Ibid., 56, 58.

42. *Back to Basics*, 84.

Chapter 9

1. Ed Webster to Dr. Bob, December 13, 1946, HPA, Box 49.

2. *Interpretation*, 35.

3. Ed Webster to Dr. Bob, May 15, 1949, HPA, Box 49.

4. McElrath, Damian, *The Essence of Twelve Step Recovery* (Center City, MN: Hazelden, 2008), 43.

5. Ed Webster to Bill W., Feb. 15, 1952, HPA, Box 49.

6. Edward A. Webster, *Stools and Bottles* (Minneapolis: Coll-Webb Co., 1961), 3rd printing, 39.

7. Ibid., 65.

8. Ibid., 53.

9. Ibid., 55.

10. Ibid., 58.

11. Ibid., 59.

12. Ibid., 61.

13. Ibid., 76.

14. *Interpretation*, 103.

15. *Interpretation*, Webster's margin notes, 103.

16. *Interpretation*, 105.

17. *Interpretation*, Webster's margin notes, 105.

18. *Interpretation*, 106.

19. *Interpretation*, Webster's margin notes, 105.

20. Ibid.

21. Ibid.

22. *Stools and Bottles*, 100.

23. Ibid., 104.

24. Ibid., 128–9.

25. Ibid., 140–1.

26. Ibid., 143.

27. Ibid., 148–9.

About the Author

Damian McElrath, D.H.E., is a researcher and historian focusing on the evolution of Alcoholics Anonymous and Twelve Step recovery. Most recently he authored *Making the Little Black Book: Inside the Working Manuscript of Twenty-Four Hours a Day,* which tells the story behind another recovery classic. His other books include *The Essence of Twelve Step Recovery: Take It to Heart* and *Hazelden: A Spiritual Odyssey*; he also wrote biographies of Pat Butler and Dan Anderson. In three decades at Hazelden in Center City, Minnesota, McElrath held a variety of positions including chaplain and, ultimately, vice president of recovery services. Before coming to Hazelden, he spent three decades as a Franciscan priest serving the spiritual needs of others through teaching, counseling, and administrative work.

Also of Interest

The Little Red Book
Own *The Little Red Book* for yourself! One of the best-loved study companions to *The Big Book of Alcoholics Anonymous*, this little volume has helped millions put the Twelve Steps to work in their daily lives. Its fund of knowledge offers support and wisdom in the search for peace of mind and contented sobriety.
Hardcover: Order no. 1030
Softcover: Order no. 1034
Ebook: EB1034

The Little Red Book for Women
Annotated by best-selling author Karen Casey, this version of the recovery classic opens new avenues of thought for women.
Hardcover: Order no. 2311
Ebook: EB2311

The Little Red Book Study Guide
BILL P.
Designed as an aid for studying *The Big Book of Alcoholics Anonymous*, this 160-page workbook also offers many helpful discussion topics for meetings.
Softcover: Order no. 1028
Ebook: Order no. EB1028

Making the Little Black Book
Inside the Working Manuscript of Twenty-Four Hours a Day
DAMIAN MCELRATH, D.H.E.

Join this beloved author in a revealing look at another recovery classic: *Twenty-Four Hours a Day.* Known widely as "the Little Black Book," it was the first meditation book written expressly for those in recovery. The original typescript, reproduced in full, shows how *Twenty-Four Hours a Day* evolved both before and after its first publication.

Hardcover: Order no. 4696
Limited collector's edition: Order no. 3986

Hazelden, a national nonprofit organization founded in 1949, helps people reclaim their lives from the disease of addiction. Built on decades of knowledge and experience, Hazelden offers a comprehensive approach to addiction that addresses the full range of patient, family, and professional needs, including treatment and continuing care for youth and adults, research, higher learning, public education and advocacy, and publishing.

A life of recovery is lived "one day at a time." Hazelden publications, both educational and inspirational, support and strengthen lifelong recovery. In 1954, Hazelden published *Twenty-Four Hours a Day,* the first daily meditation book for recovering alcoholics, and Hazelden continues to publish works to inspire and guide individuals in treatment and recovery, and their loved ones. Professionals who work to prevent and treat addiction also turn to Hazelden for evidence-based curricula, informational materials, and videos for use in schools, treatment programs, and correctional programs.

Through published works, Hazelden extends the reach of hope, encouragement, help, and support to individuals, families, and communities affected by addiction and related issues.

For questions about Hazelden publications, please call
800-328-9000
or visit us online at **hazelden.org/bookstore.**